123 Numbers, Colors, & Shapes on Parade

Preschool
Ages 3–5

March into early math concepts with fun activities
for skills such as the following:

- Numeral Recognition
- Counting
- Color Recognition
- Shape Recognition
- Sorting

Written by Jean Warren

Managing Editor: Kimberly Brugger-Murphy

Editorial Team: Becky S. Andrews, Kimberley Bruck, Karen P. Shelton,
Diane Badden, Sharon Murphy, Cindy K. Daoust, Leanne Stratton, Allison E. Ward,
Karen A. Brudnak, Sarah Hamblet, Hope Rodgers, Dorothy C. McKinney

Production Team: Lisa K. Pitts, Jennifer Tipton Cappoen (COVER ARTIST),
Pam Crane, Rebecca Saunders, Jennifer Tipton Cappoen, Chris Curry, Sarah Foreman,
Theresa Lewis Goode, Ivy L. Koonce, Clint Moore, Greg D. Rieves, Barry Slate,
Donna K. Teal, Tazmen Carlisle, Amy Kirtley-Hill, Kristy Parton, Debbie Shoffner,
Cathy Edwards Simrell, Lynette Dickerson, Mark Rainey, Kimberly Richard

Table of Contents

www.themailbox.com

©2005 The Mailbox®
All rights reserved.
ISBN# 1-56234-641-5

Manufactured in the United States
10 9 8 7 6 5 4 3 2 1

Numbers

Number 1

Decorating Number 1

This blue-ribbon idea is sure to help little ones remember the numeral 1! Make a white construction paper copy of the 1 pattern (page 50) for each child. Encourage each youngster to use crayons to embellish her number as desired. Have her cut out her pattern, providing help as needed. Then invite her to glue one length of ribbon to the cutout as shown. After the glue is dry, encourage each student to run her fingers down the ribbon while saying, "One." No doubt this idea is a winner!

There's Just One Me!

There's Just One Me

Promote self-esteem—and recognition of the numeral 1—with an art project that emphasizes youngsters' individuality! You will need a photograph of each student. To begin, give each child a large sheet of drawing paper folded in half and labeled with the title shown. Point out the word *one*. Then have each child decorate the area around the title with several colorful 1s. Next, invite her to unfold her paper and glue her picture to the left-hand side. On the right-hand side, have her draw a picture of something she enjoys. Then invite students to share their work with their classmates. With this fun project, one can't possibly be the loneliest number!

Singular Shape Hunt

Whether it's fall, winter, or spring, this small-group activity can be tailored to match any season or theme! Partially conceal around the room five different cutouts related to your current theme or the season. Gather five youngsters and invite them to search for the cutouts. After each child has found one, have him return with his cutout in hand. Then prompt each student to describe his cutout to his classmates, using the word *one* in his description. For example, a child might say, "I found one red heart cutout." After each description, lead youngsters in singing the song shown, altering the lines to reflect the gender of the child and the cutout's shape. La-la-la-lovely!

(sung to the tune of "Skip to My Lou")

He found one heart; yes, he did!
He found one heart; yes, he did!
He found one heart; yes, he did!
He found one heart today!

Rolling Ones

Your students will be on a roll with this partner game! Give a pair of youngsters a large foam die and a blank sheet of paper. Encourage the twosome to take turns rolling the die. Each time a student rolls a one, have him say, "One!" and then use a colorful crayon to write the numeral 1 on the paper. Play continues until each child has had an opportunity to write several 1s. Your little ones are sure to be game for another round!

5

One Sun

There's only one sun! Shed some light on the closest star with this stellar activity. Ask youngsters how many suns are in the sky. After they have established that there is only one sun, explain that the sun is a star. There are other stars in the sky, but they are farther away from the earth than the sun is. To help youngsters celebrate the sun, have them perform the following action poem.

One hot sun up so high,	*Hold arms in an arch above head.*
Brightly shining in the daytime sky.	*Extend arms and wiggle fingers.*
All its friends live so far,	*Place edge of hand against forehead and look left and then right.*
Like the sun, they are also stars.	*Extend arms and wiggle fingers.*

One-Cup Fruit Salad

Little ones will delight in measuring out one cup of this fruit salad, and you'll delight in how easy it is to make! Combine cans of fruit cocktail, mandarin oranges, and pineapple tidbits in a bowl. Place the resulting fruit salad at a table along with two one-cup measuring cups. Also provide a class supply of disposable bowls and plastic spoons. Invite a small group of children to the table. Have students pass around a measuring cup and identify the numeral 1 on the cup. Explain that the 1 is there to identify one cup. Then have each student use the second measuring cup to scoop one cup of salad into a bowl. Finally, give each student a spoon and have her dig in!

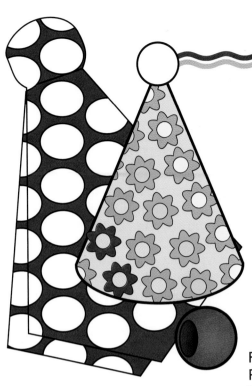

Funny Clown

You'll encourage youngsters to clown around when they perform this song about one clown and each of his silly accessories! To begin, point out one clothing item or accessory you're wearing. For example, you might say, "I am wearing one shirt." Encourage each student to follow your example and use the word *one* to describe an item he is wearing. Explain that the song they're about to sing is about a clown who is wearing one hat, one tie, and one silly red nose. Then lead youngsters in performing this fun ditty!

(sung to the tune of "This Old Man")

Funny clown, he has one   *Hold up index finger.*
Pointed hat he wears for fun.   *Hold up arms to resemble a pointed hat.*
With one giant tie   *Touch neck and then touch the floor.*
And one silly red nose,   *Touch nose.*
He likes to dance on his toes!   *Dance around on toes.*

One Little Egg

Little ones are sure to come out of their shells when you reinforce the numeral 1 with this "egg-citing" poem! Have each youngster draw the numeral 1 on a colorful egg cutout. Then encourage him to tape the cutout to a craft stick to make a stick puppet. Have each student sit in a circle in your large-group area with his puppet in hand. Then lead youngsters in reciting the poem, encouraging them to raise their puppets each time they say, "One little egg." After the performance, ask students why they think the egg begins to cheep at the end of the poem.

One little egg sitting on the wall.
One little egg tips and falls.
One little egg rolls down the street.
One little egg starts to cheep!

Cheep! Cheep!

7

Number 2

Decorating Number 2

Clouds really can take the shape of anything—even the numeral 2! Use the pattern on page 51 to make a white construction paper 2 cutout for each child. Have her trace the numeral with her finger and say the word *two*. Invite her to count two cotton balls and glue them to the numeral. Display the resulting projects on a blue bulletin board. If desired, add a sun cutout and several cloud cutouts to the board. Cloud gazing is "two" much fun!

Mitten Pairs

The result of this project is a handsome hanging display that helps youngsters practice counting to two! Make two white construction paper copies of the mitten pattern on page 52 for each child. Have each student use crayons to embellish the mittens as desired. Then encourage him to cut them out, providing help as necessary. Next, hole-punch the mittens and tie them to opposite ends of a length of yarn. Suspend these wintry creations from your classroom ceiling as shown. Then have youngsters count to two as you point to each pair!

Two Red Apples

With this "tree-mendously" fun collage activity, youngsters discover that a pair means two similar items! Using the patterns on page 53, make a brown construction paper tree cutout and two red construction paper apple cutouts for each child. Have each student glue green construction paper squares to the tree cutout to resemble foliage. Then encourage her to glue each apple to the tree. Next, explain that the tree has a pair of apples and the word *pair* means two similar items. Have each child count the apples orally to confirm that there are two. That's one for me and one for you!

It's a Match!

Look no further than your collection of winter accessories to find props for this handy matching center! Collect several pairs of matching mittens and gloves. Place the pairs in a container and set the container in a center. Also place in the center a supply of index cards labeled with the numeral 2. A child visits the center, removes the mittens and gloves from the container, and matches the pairs. Then she places a card on top of each pair!

From One to Two

It's easy for students to transform one snack into two when the treat for the day is graham crackers! Give each youngster a square of graham cracker made up of two connected rectangles. Have each child break his graham cracker into two pieces. Encourage him to count the pieces as he points to each one. If desired, give each youngster a small amount of frosting or strawberry cream cheese to spread on his crackers. Then have him nibble on his tasty treat!

Measuring Liquids

With this whole-group measurement activity, youngsters discover that two is a very important number! Obtain the following plastic containers: a one-cup measuring cup, a pint container, and a quart container. Place them in your large-group area with a container of water. Ask youngsters how many cups of water they think will fit into the pint container. After listening to several predictions, have youngsters count as you pour cups of water into the container. Repeat the process, asking youngsters how many pints of water will fit into the quart container. Youngsters will be surprised to find that in both cases the answer is two! If desired, place the containers at your water table for independent exploration.

Two Little Blackbirds

When you combine two puppet props with this traditional rhyme the result is a kid-pleasing performance! To begin, help each youngster make two simple blackbird stick puppets similar to the ones shown. (Use the pattern on page 107 if desired.) Have each youngster hold a puppet in each hand. Then lead the class in performing the poem.

Two little blackbirds sitting on a hill, One named Jack and one named Jill.	*Hold up both puppets.* *Raise one puppet; then the other.*
Fly away Jack; fly away Jill.	*Move one puppet behind your back; then move the other behind your back.*
Come back Jack; come back Jill.	*Reveal one puppet; then reveal the other puppet.*

A Book of 2s

Youngsters will be seeing double when they make these entertaining booklets! Give each youngster a booklet with a cover titled "My Book of 2s" and four blank pages. Have each child think of his favorite animal. Then encourage him to draw the animal twice on the first page of his booklet. Have each student label his pictures or have him dictate the information as you label the pictures. Continue in the same fashion with each remaining page, choosing categories such as his favorite food, his favorite shape, and his favorite toy. When the booklet is finished, have him take it home to share with his family.

Number 3

***

Decorating Number 3

What shape is well-known for its connection to the number 3? Why, the triangle, of course! With this activity, youngsters decorate the numeral 3 with three colorful triangles. Give each child a white construction paper copy of the 3 pattern (page 54). Have each youngster color the three as desired. Then give her three colorful triangle cutouts and encourage her to glue them to the 3. Have each youngster count the points on each triangle. Then encourage her to count all the triangles. She's sure to say, "I see three!"

***

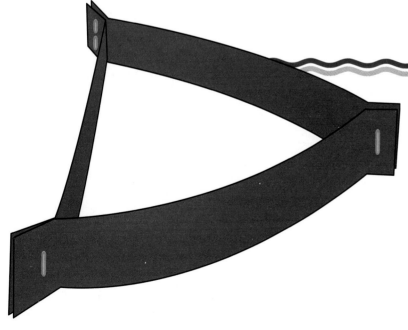

Three-Cornered Hats

This fun headwear has three corners! To make a three-cornered hat for each child, staple together three 2" x 12" construction paper strips as shown. Give each child a hat and explain that the hats are called three-cornered hats. Ask youngsters why they think the hats have been given that name. After they establish that the hat has three corners, have each child count orally as she touches each corner. Next, invite her to don her hat. (If the hat fits too loosely, place additional staples further from the ends.) Then give her a small cup of triangular crackers to nibble on. The crackers have three corners just like the hat!

On a Roll

You can count on this small-group game being a hit with your little ones! Gather a group of three students and give them a large foam die and nine cards labeled with the numeral 3. Have the students take turns rolling the die. Each time a child rolls a three, encourage him to take a card. Play continues until each child earns three cards. Everybody wins with this entertaining game!

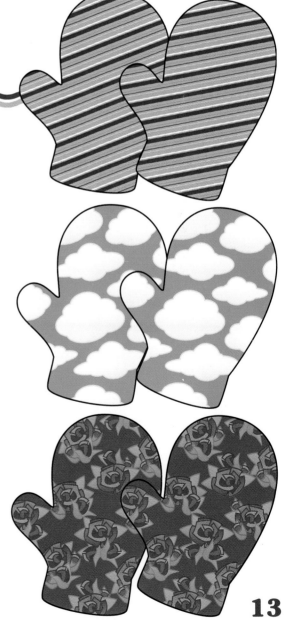

Three Little Kittens

When your youngsters pretend to be the three little kittens with this small-group activity, they're sure to be eager to look for their lost mittens! Purchase a class supply of small snacks. Cut three pairs of mitten shapes from different wallpaper samples. Then partially conceal in the classroom one mitten from each pair. To begin, gather three children and give each child one of the remaining mittens. Begin reciting the traditional rhyme "The Three Little Kittens," stopping directly after the mother cat scolds the kittens for losing their mittens. Then explain to the students that they are going to pretend to be the three little kittens. Count the students aloud. Then have each child search for the mate to his mitten. When all three children return with their mittens, recite the rest of the rhyme. Then ask the students how many pieces of pie are needed for the kittens. After it is established that three pieces are needed, count out three snacks with your youngsters and give one to each child.

Rub-A-Dub-Dub

Who's in the tub? Your little ones will be delighted when they practice counting to three with this twist on a traditional rhyme. Obtain an empty margarine tub. Also gather three toy people and four other sets of three small items, such as toy dinosaurs, blocks, and toy cars. To begin, have youngsters count as you place three toy people in the tub. Then teach youngsters the traditional rhyme "Rub-A-Dub-Dub, Three Men in a Tub." Next, remove the people and have students count aloud as you replace them with a set of three other objects. Then have them repeat the rhyme, substituting the word *men* with the name of the new objects in the tub. Continue in the same way with each set of three items, prompting youngsters to count the objects before each recitation. If desired, place the objects and the tub at your water table for independent exploration. Rub-a-dub-dub, three dinosaurs in a tub!

Sandwich Stackers

Youngsters build a mini sandwich with three items for this fun snack session. Gather a small group of children at a table and give each child a plastic knife and a paper plate with one-half of a slice of bread. Each child cuts the bread in half again. He uses a squeeze-style condiment, such as ketchup, mustard, or mayonnaise, to make the numeral 3 on a piece of his bread. Then he chooses three sandwich fillings of his choice, such as cheese, ham, and turkey, and counts aloud as he places the items on his bread. After he tops the sandwich with the remaining piece of bread, he eats his tasty sandwich stack!

Three Wishes

When youngsters listen to a read-aloud of this folktale, they'll certainly be eager to make a booklet with three wishes of their own! Read aloud a version of the folktale *The Three Wishes.* Then give each child a booklet with a cover titled "My _____ Wishes" and three pages labeled with the prompt "I wish." Have each child write the numeral 3 in the blank on the cover. Then encourage him to write his name under the title. Invite each student to think of three wishes he would ask for if he had the opportunity. Have him write (or dictate as you write) a wish on each page and then draw a picture to match. What wonderful wishes!

I wish that I had a green bicycle.

Play Dough 3s

Rolling, shaping, squishing—making 3s with a supply of colorful play dough is fun! Label each of four sheets of tagboard with the numeral 3. Laminate the tagboard for durability and then place the resulting workmat at a table with a supply of colorful play dough. Invite up to four students to the table and give each child a workmat. Encourage her to roll a piece of play dough into a long snake. Then have her arrange the play dough in the shape of a 3 on the workmat, using the written numeral as a guide. When youngsters are comfortable with this activity, encourage them to form 3s with play dough without using the workmat.

Number 4

Decorating Number 4

With this fun activity, youngsters dress up the numeral 4 with colorful cutouts! Make a white construction paper copy of the 4 pattern (page 55) for each child. Gather a supply of cutouts in two different seasonal shapes. To begin, have each child color a four pattern. Then encourage her to pick one of the two seasonal shapes. After she counts four of the corresponding cutouts, invite her to glue them around her pattern. There are four pumpkins!

Fabulous Frames

What can a youngster make with four jumbo craft sticks? A frame for the numeral 4! Gather four jumbo craft sticks for each child. Make a class supply of tagboard squares whose sides are each the same length as a craft stick. To begin, give each child a piece of tagboard and have her use a colorful marker to write the numeral 4 in the center. Invite her to place four mini stickers around the numeral. Next, give each child four craft sticks and have her count them aloud. Help her glue a stick to each side of the square to resemble a frame. When the glue is dry, encourage her to take her project home to share with her family. This idea is sure to help little ones picture the numeral 4!

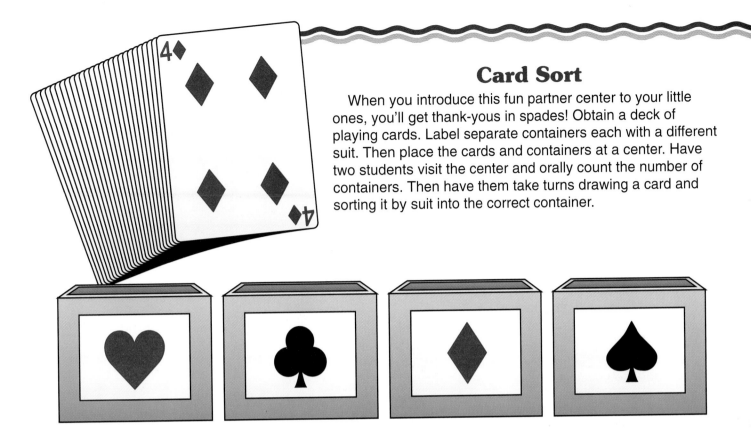

Card Sort

When you introduce this fun partner center to your little ones, you'll get thank-yous in spades! Obtain a deck of playing cards. Label separate containers each with a different suit. Then place the cards and containers at a center. Have two students visit the center and orally count the number of containers. Then have them take turns drawing a card and sorting it by suit into the correct container.

Four Colors Game

This colorful whole-group game is sure to get repeated requests! Cut a square from each of the following colors of construction paper: red, blue, yellow, and green. Post a different square in each corner of your room. To make a game spinner, divide a tagboard circle into four sections. Color the sections to reflect the colors of the squares. To begin, stand with your youngsters in the center of the room. Count aloud with students as you point to each colored square. Then invite each child to choose a square and stand near it. Using a pencil and a paper clip, spin the spinner as shown and then name the color. Encourage youngsters standing near the corresponding square to sit with you in the center of the room. Give the remaining students a chance to either stay where they are or choose a new square before spinning again. After a few rounds, invite youngsters sitting with you to reenter the game!

Four Seasons

Watch youngsters blossom as they decorate these bare trees to match the four seasons. Draw four simple tree shapes on a length of bulletin board paper. Then display the paper on a wall in your classroom. To begin, count the trees with your youngsters. After establishing that there are four trees, explain that there is one tree for each season. Depending on student level, you may wish to have children volunteer information about the four seasons. Label each tree with the name of a different season. Next, for each of four consecutive school days, have students decorate a different tree (see decorating suggestions below). This display is sure to catch the eye of anyone who visits your classroom!

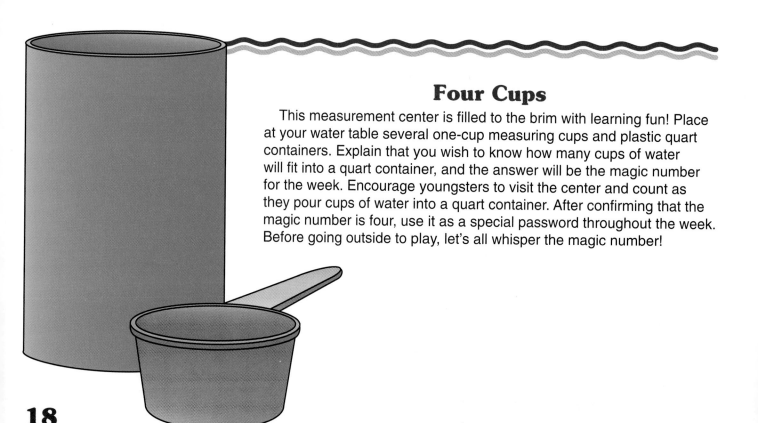

Fall   Winter   Spring   Summer

Suggestions for decorating each tree:
Fall: Glue on fall-colored leaf cutouts.
Winter: Glue on pieces of cotton batting (snow).
Spring: Glue on crumpled squares of pink tissue paper (blossoms).
Summer: Glue on green leaf cutouts.

Four Cups

This measurement center is filled to the brim with learning fun! Place at your water table several one-cup measuring cups and plastic quart containers. Explain that you wish to know how many cups of water will fit into a quart container, and the answer will be the magic number for the week. Encourage youngsters to visit the center and count as they pour cups of water into a quart container. After confirming that the magic number is four, use it as a special password throughout the week. Before going outside to play, let's all whisper the magic number!

18

Four Little Turtles

This poem about four little sea turtles goes swimmingly with playful flannelboard props! Ready four turtle cutouts for flannelboard use. (If desired, use the pattern on page 108.) Gather youngsters around and place the cutouts on the left-hand side of your flannelboard. Begin reciting the poem shown, moving each turtle to the right-hand side of the flannelboard when indicated and encouraging youngsters to supply the numeral at the end of each couplet. For the final couplet, move the last turtle over to find all three of its missing friends!

Four little turtles float in the sea.
One goes home, and that leaves three.

Three little turtles bob in the blue.
One goes home, and that leaves two.

Two little turtles swim in the sun.
One goes home and that leaves one.

One little turtle swims near the ocean floor.
It found its friends, and now there are four!

Four Seasons Riddle

Focus little ones' attention on this four seasons center with an engaging riddle! Make a brown construction paper tree cutout. Laminate the cutout for durability and then place it at a center along with blossom cutouts, green leaf cutouts, and fall-colored leaf cutouts. Read the riddle shown and have youngsters guess the answer. After establishing that the riddle is describing a tree, invite two youngsters to the center. Ask the students to name the four seasons. Next, encourage one child to close his eyes while his partner places cutouts on the tree so that it resembles a specific season. (To show winter, the child would leave the tree bare.) When he's finished arranging the cutouts, encourage his partner to open his eyes, look at the tree, and guess the season. Have him remove the cutouts. Then encourage the students to switch roles. That's "unbe-leaf-ably" fun!

In winter, I'm as bare as bare can be.
In spring, I'm covered with blossoms and bees.
In summer, I'm filled with leaves so green.
In fall, my leaves are the prettiest you've seen.

19

Number 5

Decorating Number 5

These illuminating numerals reinforce the concept of the numeral 5! Use the pattern on page 56 to make a black construction paper 5 cutout for each child. Place the cutouts at a table along with a shallow pan of white tempera paint and a sponge trimmed in the shape of a small star. Invite a child to the table and encourage him to press the star in the paint and then print five stars on a cutout. If desired, have each student sprinkle fine glitter over the paint. When his cutout is dry, encourage him to glue it onto a 9" x 12" sheet of colorful construction paper. Display these sparkling 5s in the classroom!

A Starry Night

Youngsters practice writing the numeral 5 to make this star-studded mural! Give each youngster in a small group a yellow star cutout labeled with the numeral 5. Encourage each child to count the points on the star. Then have him trace the numeral with his finger while he says, "Five." Next, encourage each student to trace over the number with glitter glue. After the glue is dry, tape the finished stars to a length of black bulletin board paper and then display the resulting mural on a wall in the classroom. What a lovely starry night!

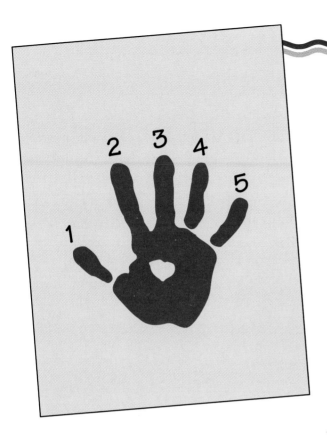

Handprints

Students will want to give themselves a hand after this printmaking activity! Invite each student to make a colorful handprint of his right hand on a sheet of light-colored construction paper. When the paint is dry, use a black marker to number the digits 1 through 5, beginning with the thumb. Give each child his handprint and have him count aloud as he touches the thumb and then each finger. One, two, three, four, five!

Grouping by Fives

Grouping objects by fives is a snap with a supply of small blocks. Label each of five paper plates with the numeral 5. Place the plates at a center along with 25 small blocks. A student visits the center. She counts out groups of five blocks and places each group on a different paper plate. That's five servings of counting practice coming right up!

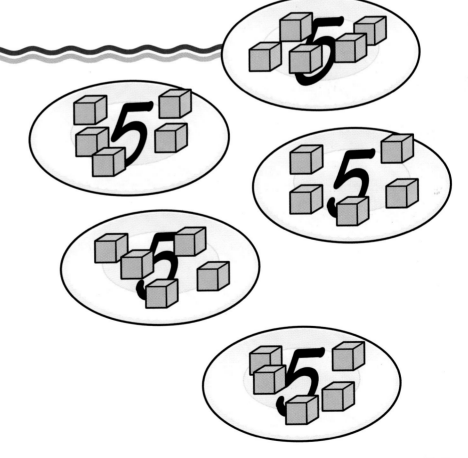

The Five Senses

This citrusy idea has little ones using their five senses to explore a popular fruit! Label a piece of chart paper with each of the five senses, leaving space after each one. Arrange youngsters in a circle in your large-group area. Explain that people use the senses to learn about the world around them. Count the senses on the chart with your youngsters. After establishing that there are five, present an orange. Have youngsters look at the orange and describe what they see; write each child's words in the appropriate location on the paper. Continue in a similar way for the senses of touch and hearing, having youngsters feel the orange and then having them listen to the orange being peeled. Finally, give each child an orange section and have him smell it. After writing down descriptive words for the orange's smell, invite each child to eat his orange section. Then complete the chart by writing youngsters' descriptions of the orange's taste. That's sensational!

see: orange, round, shiny

touch: bumpy

hear: tearing, ripping

smell: like juice, fresh

taste: sweet, yummy

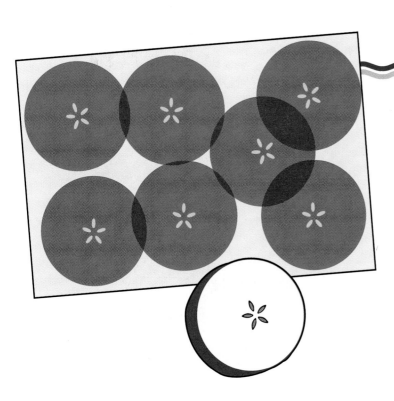

Five-Star Seed Prints

Your little ones will be stunned to discover that there is a five-pointed star hiding in the middle of every apple! Present an apple to your youngsters and ask them what they would find inside if it were sliced open. After they voice several suggestions, ask them whether they have ever seen a star inside an apple. Cut the apple in half horizontally. Then, with much fanfare, show youngsters the star pattern of the seeds. Explain that a star has five points and then have youngsters count aloud to five. Next, invite a small group of students to your art center. Have each child press the cut side of an apple into a shallow pan of colorful tempera paint. Then encourage him to gently press it onto a 12" x 18" sheet of construction paper. Invite him to repeat the process until a desired effect is achieved. After the paint is dry, display these stellar prints in the classroom!

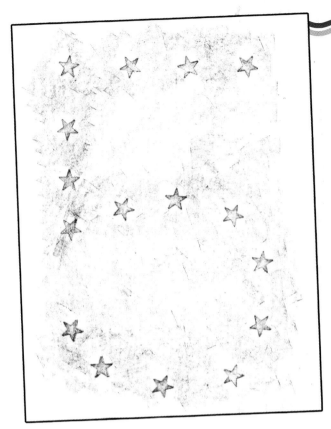

Number 5 Rubbings

When youngsters go stargazing at this center, they make rubbings in the shape of the numeral 5! Affix star stickers in the shape of the numeral 5 to a transparency sheet. Securely tape the sheet to a table. Then place at the table a supply of copy paper and several crayons with their wrappers removed. Encourage a youngster to visit the table. Have him run his fingers over the numeral and say its name. Then have him place a sheet of copy paper over a prepared transparency. Encourage the child to rub the side of a crayon over the paper until the number is revealed. That's amazing!

Five Little Frogs

Your little ones will be hopping with excitement to perform this fun froggy fingerplay! Lead youngsters in reciting the poem several times. When they are comfortable reciting the words, encourage them to add the actions provided.

Five little frogs hopped on a log	*Hold up five fingers; then hop in place.*
To see what they could see.	*Place edge of hand against forehead and look left and then right.*
The first one saw five dragonflies.	*Point to your thumb.*
The second one saw five trees.	*Point to your first finger.*
The third one saw five butterflies	*Point to your second finger.*
Fluttering around so free.	*Flutter both hands to resemble wings.*
The fourth one saw five lily pads.	*Point to your third finger.*
The fifth one saw five bees.	*Point to your fourth finger.*

Number 6

Decorating Number 6

Youngsters are sure to have a picnic decorating the numeral 6 with six fingerprint ants! Use the pattern on page 57 to make a white construction paper 6 cutout for each child. Invite a student to your art area. Encourage her to press a finger into a shallow pan of black tempera paint. Then have her make six sets of three fingerprints on her cutout to resemble ants, adding more paint to her finger as needed. After the paint dries, encourage each child to use a thin black marker to make six legs on each ant. Mount each cutout on a 9" x 12" sheet of red construction paper. Then display the completed project on a bulletin board to resemble a picnic blanket. These ants go marching six by six!

Flower Pictures

Little ones' number skills bloom when they count to six to make these lovely flowers! Encourage each child to write the numeral 6 on a yellow circle cutout and then glue it to the middle of a 9" x 12" sheet of green construction paper. Have him count six colorful petal cutouts and then glue them around the circle. Then have each youngster take his finished project home to share with his family!

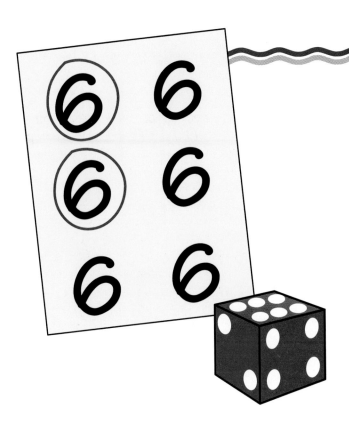

A Dice Game

Your little ones will be experts at spotting sets of six when they visit this partner center! Write the numeral 6 on a sheet of paper six times. Then make a copy for every two students. Place the sheets at a center along with a large foam die. Two youngsters visit the center and a child rolls the die. If he rolls a six, his partner circles one of the numerals on the sheet. If he rolls a different number, his partner does nothing. The students repeat the process, taking turns rolling the die until each 6 is circled!

Muffin Tin Toss

Bring a muffin tin out of the kitchen and into the classroom for an engaging game that focuses on the number six! Place a six-cup muffin tin at a table. Invite a small group of youngsters to the table and encourage them to orally count the cups. After establishing that there are six cups, give each student six medium-size pom-poms. Have each child orally count his pom-poms. Next, place the tin near the edge of the table. Invite the students to line up in front of the tin. Then encourage each child, in turn, to toss his pom-poms into the muffin tin, with the goal of getting one in each cup. After he has tossed all six pom-poms, have him remove them from the cups. What fun!

Insect Investigation

Youngsters get a leg up on counting to six when they make these artsy insects! Provide access to a variety of craft supplies, such as wallpaper samples, pom-poms, and tissue paper scraps. Encourage each child to design an insect's body by gluing craft supplies to a sheet of colorful construction paper. After each student has finished the body, give her six construction paper strips to represent legs. Encourage each child to orally count the strips. Then have her glue three strips on each side of the insect. After the glue is dry, display these creative critters in your classroom!

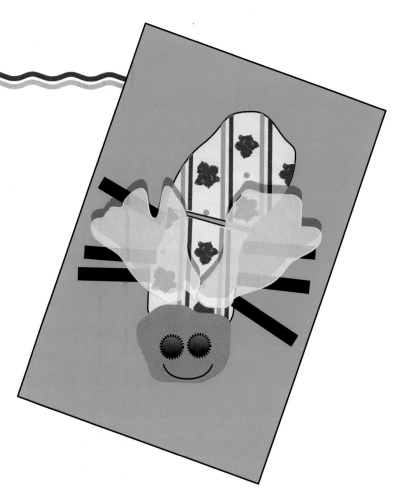

Six-Legged Snack

How many legs do youngsters place on this insect snack? Why, six, of course! A youngster places three circular crackers (body parts) on a plate. She uses spreadable cheese to attach two Crispix cereal pieces (eyes). Then the child places two thin apple slices (wings) on top of the crackers. Next, she counts six pretzel sticks (legs) and places three on each side of the body. Finally, invite youngsters to nibble on their crunchy critters!

Six Gumballs

Youngsters will have a ball when they recite this poem about six gumballs! To make flannelboard props, cut a piece of felt in the shape of a gumball machine. Make a construction paper gumball from each of the following colors: yellow, blue, purple, red, orange, and green. Draw a happy face on each gumball and then ready the gumballs for flannelboard use. Place the cutouts on a flannelboard as shown. Lead children in reciting the rhyme shown six times, removing one gumball each time and encouraging youngsters to count the number of gumballs remaining after each repetition.

[Six] gumballs in a gumball machine—
Yellow, blue, purple, red, orange, and green.
Clatter, clatter, clank—someone's dime goes in,
And one gumball leaves with a happy grin.
I'll count the gumballs that I see
To find out how many are left for me!

Six Little Songbirds

Birds of a feather sing together about the number six! Invite six youngsters to pretend to be birds and have them stand in a row. Count the birds with the remaining students. Then lead the class in singing the song shown.

(sung to the tune of "Six Little Ducks")

Six little songbirds in a tree,
Singing their song so merrily.
They sing for the spring, and they sing for the sun.
They sing for me and sing for everyone,
Everyone, everyone.
They sing for me and sing for everyone!

Number 7

Decorating Number 7

Butterflies! Pumpkins! Snowflakes! When youngsters stamp seven images on the numeral 7, the possibilities are endless! Use the pattern on page 58 to make a white construction paper 7 cutout for each child. Place the cutouts at a table along with a rubber stamp and an ink pad. Invite a child to the table and have him count aloud as he stamps seven images on a cutout. Encourage him to glue his cutout to a 9" x 12" sheet of colorful construction paper. Then display these stamped sevens in the classroom!

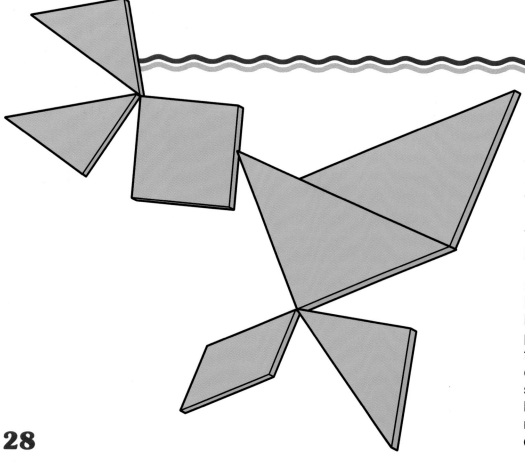

Terrific Tangrams

Youngsters' imaginations soar when they explore a tangram! Use the pattern on page 59 to make a set of construction paper tangram pieces for each child. Place each set in a resealable plastic bag. Have each student open his bag, remove the pieces, and then count them aloud. After he establishes that there are seven pieces, encourage him to arrange them to make a design. It's a dinosaur!

Seven!

Seven in the Circle

Seven is the magic number in this fun circle-time game! Have youngsters sit in a circle in your large-group area. Encourage them to count aloud as they pass a ball around the circle. When they reach the number seven, the child who is holding the ball gives it to the next student and then sits in the middle of the circle. The youngsters repeat the process until seven children are seated in the middle. The remaining students orally count the group of seven. Then the children rejoin the circle for another round!

Seven Sillies

Your youngsters will be the first to tell you that it's fun to act silly. So they will be overjoyed when you encourage silly behavior with this playful chant! Practice counting to seven with your youngsters. Then explain that the poem they are about to perform is about seven people who act very silly. Lead youngsters in reciting the rhyme, encouraging them to act out the words!

Seven sillies went to town,
Flapping their arms up and down,
Hopping on the left foot and then on the right,
Stubbing their toes in broad daylight.

Seven sillies bought seven cars.
They pushed them home—it wasn't far.
Seven sillies jumped in bed.
They jumped so high, they bumped their heads!

Seven Days of the Week

This idea will be a pleasing addition to your daily calendar time! Gather youngsters around your monthly calendar and point out that each week has seven days. Count with your youngsters the days in each full week. Then encourage students to sing the song shown to help them remember the seven days of the week.

(sung to the tune of "Are You Sleeping?")

Monday, Tuesday,
Monday, Tuesday,
Wednesday, Thursday,
Wednesday, Thursday,
Friday, Saturday, Sunday,
Friday, Saturday, Sunday—
Seven days
Of the week.

JUNE

Sunday	Monday	Tuesday	Wednesday	Thursday	Friday	Saturday
			1	2	3	4
5	6	7	8	9	10	11
12	13	14	15	16	17	18
19	20	21	22	23	24	25
26	27	28	29	30		

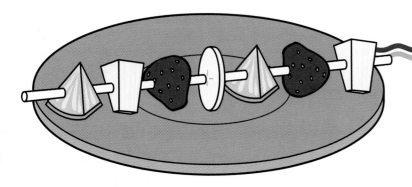

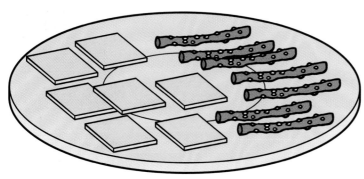

Savory Seven

Try one or both of these tasty treats to reinforce the concept of the number seven!

- Make fruit kabobs with your youngsters by encouraging them to slide seven small slices of fruit—such as oranges, bananas, and strawberries—onto a drinking straw. Encourage each child to count the fruit slices; then have her dig in!
- Give each student seven pretzel sticks and seven small pieces of cheese. Encourage each youngster to count the sticks and then count the cheese slices to ensure that there are seven of each. Then have him gently stab a pretzel stick into each cheese slice before munching on his treat!

Seven Sailors

Ahoy there! With this small-group activity, your little ones give a ship to each of seven toy sailors. Gather seven children around your water table. Have youngsters count with you as you place seven plastic containers (boats) in the water. Then have them count again as you give each child a plastic toy person. Encourage each student to place his person in a boat. Then lead youngsters in reciting the rhyme shown. If desired, leave the items at the water table for youngsters to explore during center time. This idea is sure to make a splash!

Seven ships upon the sea
With seven sailors, hi-dee-dee!
Sailing fast and sailing free,
Seven sailors, hi-dee-dee!

Writing 7s

Little hands will appreciate writing the numeral 7 in a tray full of rice! Spread a thin layer of rice in a plastic tray. Place the tray at a table and then invite a youngster to join you. Encourage the child to use his finger to write the numeral 7 in the rice. (You may wish to have a written 7 for youngsters to use as a reference.) Shake the tray gently, and the student is ready to make another 7! Rice is nice!

Number 8

Decorating Number 8

How do students know that the critters on these cutouts are spiders? Because of their eight legs, of course! Invite a small group of children to a table and give each youngster a colorful construction paper copy of the 8 pattern (page 60). Have him trace the numeral with his finger and say, "Eight." Then provide access to a black ink pad and have him make eight fingerprints on the numeral. Encourage him to use a fine-tip black marker to add eight legs to each fingerprint to resemble a spider. When these splendid spider projects are finished, have little ones take them home to share with their families.

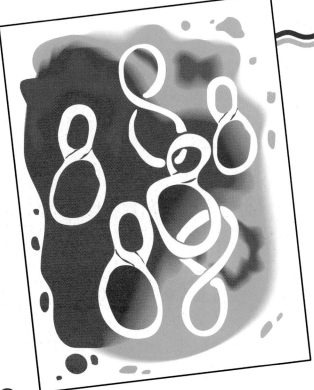

Fingerpainting Eights

Youngsters won't have to don ice skates to make these figure eights! Explain that ice skaters can sometimes be seen skating in the shape of the numeral 8. Give each child a large sheet of white paper. Then place two different colors of fingerpaint on the paper. Encourage each student to pretend his fingers are skates as he moves them through the paint to make figure eights. After the paint is dry, display the paintings on a bulletin board. That's some fancy finger skating!

Spiders

These three-dimensional spiders and their eight bendable legs are sure to thrill your little ones! Obtain enough black Crayola Model Magic (or another kind of self-hardening modeling material) for each child to have a small ball plus extra for facial features. Encourage each youngster to slightly flatten her ball of clay to represent a spider's body. Give each child eight black six-inch chenille stems and encourage her to count them aloud. Have her push the end of each chenille stem into the ball to resemble legs. Then encourage her to use additional modeling material to make any desired features and press them onto the spider. Follow the package directions for drying the project. Then have youngsters bend the legs as shown. Display these eight-legged critters in the classroom.

Eight-Sided Signs

Little ones will enjoy playing this whole-group game so much that they won't want to stop! Use the pattern on page 106 to make a stop sign and a go sign similar to the ones shown. Then present the signs to your youngsters. Explain that each sign is in the shape of an octagon and that an octagon has eight sides. Have youngsters count aloud as you point to each side of a sign. Next, hold up the go sign and invite students to quietly walk around the room. After several seconds, hold up the stop sign and encourage youngsters to stop. Continue in the same way, prompting students to watch carefully and stop as soon as you hold up the stop sign. Your little ones' grins are a sign that they enjoy this activity!

Octopus Discovery

Little ones identify facts about a well-known eight-legged creature with this whole-group activity! On a large sheet of paper, make a simple octopus drawing similar to the one shown. Post the paper in your large-group area. To begin, prompt youngsters to identify the animal on the paper. Then orally count the arms with your students. Next, read aloud a nonfiction book about octopuses. When you are finished reading, ask youngsters to share something they learned from the book. Write the statements on index cards and then tape the cards to the arms of the octopus. What a fascinating creature!

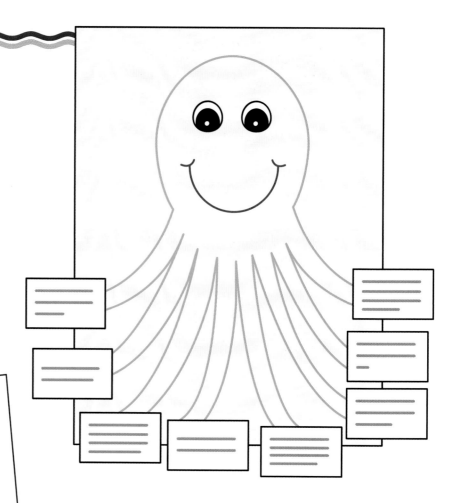

If an octopus loses an arm, it grows another one!

Eat an Eight

This tasty treat helps youngsters understand the concept of the number eight. Each student places two halves of a mini bagel on a plate to resemble the numeral 8. She spreads strawberry cream cheese on each half. Then she counts eight M&M's Minis candies and places them on the 8. Hey, this tastes great!

My Stop Sign

Youngsters hold their own stop sign props when they recite this nifty rhyme! Give each student a red square with a diagonal line drawn across each corner as shown. Encourage him to follow the lines with his scissors to cut off the corners. Then prompt each youngster to count the sides of the resulting octagon. After he determines that there are eight sides, encourage him to write the word *stop* on the octagon. Then help him tape a jumbo craft stick to the back to resemble a stop sign. (Be sure to make a sign for yourself.) Next, begin reciting the rhyme shown with your students, holding up your stop sign during the first and third couplets and encouraging students to hold up their signs during the second and fourth couplets.

My stop sign has eight sides.
It's an octagon shape.

My stop sign has eight sides.
I think it's really great.

My stop sign has eight sides.
I hold it up, you see.

My stop sign has eight sides,
And people stop for me!

Writing 8s

Little ones practice writing the numeral 8 at this sandy center! Place two craft sticks at your sand table and invite two youngsters to the table. Have them use the edge of a craft stick to smooth out the sand. Then encourage each child to use a stick to "write" 8s in the sand. What fun!

Number 9

Decorating Number 9

These 9s are so unique and colorful, your youngsters will want to display them for all to see! Use the pattern on page 61 to make a colorful construction paper 9 cutout for each child. Encourage each youngster to hole-punch nine holes in the cutout, saving the dots for later use. (If desired, have youngsters use a shape puncher.) Invite her to glue her cutout to a 9" x 12" sheet of construction paper in a contrasting color. Then have her glue her nine dots around the numeral.

Number 9 Shakers

Your little music makers will just love these nine-bean shakers! Invite a small group of students to a table and encourage them to count as each of them places nine dried kidney beans in a separate plastic disposable cup. For each child, place a second cup on top of the first, as shown, and tape the cups together. Then encourage youngsters to use the resulting shakers during music activities. When they are finished using the shakers, store them until the next musical experience. Shake, shake, shake!

Groups of Nine

With this "berry" fun partner activity, youngsters find different ways to divide nine berries! Make two green bush cutouts and place them at a table along with nine blue pom-poms (blueberries). Invite two youngsters to a table and encourage one child to divide the berries as desired between the two bushes. Have her count the number of berries on each bush; then have her combine the berries and count the total. Challenge her partner to repeat the process, dividing the nine berries a different way. Continue in the same way, having youngsters take turns until they have demonstrated several ways to divide the berries. One bush has seven berries, and the other bush has two berries. When they're combined, that makes nine berries!

Nine-Hole Golf

What do you get when you combine croquet with golf? This playful outdoor game, which helps little ones identify numerals from 1 to 9! In advance, label each of nine croquet wickets with a different numeral from 1 to 9. Then arrange the wickets in your outdoor play area. Provide access to several small balls. Have a child choose a ball. Then encourage her to say the word *one* as she rolls her ball through wicket number 1. Have her continue in the same way, rolling the ball through the remaining wickets in sequential order. No doubt this active game will be a favorite!

Nine Planets

When youngsters learn about the nine planets with this activity, they're sure to say, "Outer space is a fascinating place!" Gather youngsters in your large-group area and explain that our planet is part of a group of nine planets that move around the sun. Have youngsters practice counting to nine. Show them pictures of the planets from nonfiction books or magazines. Then sing the song shown, ending with a recitation of the names of the nine planets. (Depending on student ability, you may wish to teach youngsters the song and the names of the planets.)

(sung to the tune of "Twinkle, Twinkle, Little Star")

There's nine planets and a star
In this solar system of ours.
Each one has a special name.
No two planets are the same.
If you listen, I will say
All their names for you today!

Mercury, Venus, Earth, Mars, Jupiter, Saturn, Uranus,
    Neptune, Pluto

Number Nine Snack Mix

Nine cereal pieces, nine pretzels, and nine crackers—now that sounds like a tasty snack mix! Place several small snack items, such as those mentioned above, in separate dishes at a table. Invite a small group of students to the table and give each child a resealable plastic bag. Encourage each youngster to count nine of each type of snack and place them in her bag. After she is finished counting, invite her to nibble on her bag of treats!

Nine Baseball Players

No doubt this whole-group activity will be a hit with your little ones! Write the numeral 9 on your board. Then have youngsters identify the numeral. Explain that nine is an important number in a popular sport. Encourage students to guess which sport you might be talking about. After they determine that the sport is baseball, explain that there are nine players on a baseball team. Then lead youngsters in singing the following song.

(sung to the tune of "Three Blind Mice")

Nine baseball players,
Nine baseball players,
Playing on a team,
Playing on a team.
See the players who hit home runs.
See how they play till their game is done.
They like to play; it's a lot of fun—
Nine baseball players.

A Picnic for Nine

How many hamburgers are needed for a nine-person picnic? Your little ones will let you know with this nifty learning opportunity! Post a sheet of chart paper in your large-group area. Then explain that you are inviting nine people to a picnic and you need to make a list to make sure the guests each get one of each type of food. As a child suggests a food item, prompt her to be specific and mention how many will be needed to feed nine people. Then write her suggestion on the chart paper. Continue in the same way, prompting youngsters to mention different picnic foods. When the list contains several items, read it aloud with your children. What a tasty sounding menu!

9 hamburgers
9 hot dogs
9 bananas
9 bowls of ice cream
9 cupcakes
9 pickles
9 glasses of lemonade

Number *10*

Decorating Number 10

Here's a handy idea for decorating the numeral 10! For each child, make a copy of the 1 and 0 patterns (pages 50 and 62) onto colorful construction paper. Have each student glue the cutouts to the upper portion of a 12" x 18" sheet of construction paper to make the numeral 10. Next, have him gently press his hands in a shallow pan of colorful tempera paint. Encourage him to make handprints under the 10 as shown. After the paint is dry, have each youngster identify the numeral and then count the thumbs and fingers on his handprints. There are ten!

Ten Triangles

This counting center is "dino-mite"! Draw a simple stegosaurus outline on copy paper. Then make three green construction paper copies. Cut out the patterns and mount them on contrasting paper. Make 30 green triangle cutouts. Laminate the dinosaurs and the triangles and place them at a center. A child counts as he places ten triangles on each dinosaur's back to resemble plates. Your little ones will roar with approval!

Tenpin Bowling

There's fun to spare with this tenpin bowling game! Remove the labels from ten empty 20-ounce plastic soda bottles. Partially fill each bottle with sand, secure its lid, and then tape the lid in place. Cut ten colorful circles from construction paper. Then use clear Con-Tact covering to attach the circles to the floor in the arrangement shown. Place a bottle on each circle. To begin, invite a child to the area and encourage her to roll a medium-size ball toward the pins. Have her count the pins that were knocked down. Then, after she places the fallen pins back on the circles, invite her to count all ten pins!

Ten Pennies

This partner activity is rich in counting skills! In advance, obtain 60 paper or tagboard penny manipulatives and make six pink piggy bank cutouts. To begin, gather two students and present the pennies. Explain that you are trying to find out how many groups of ten pennies you have. Have each child, in turn, count ten pennies and place them on a piggy bank. Have the pair continue in the same way until each bank has ten pennies. Encourage the youngsters to count the groups of ten. Neat!

41

Crab Legs

Little ones count ten legs to make these cute crustaceans! Give each youngster a small red paper plate (or have students cover a small white paper plate with red paint). Then give her ten red construction paper strips (legs). Encourage her to count the legs. After she determines that there are ten legs, invite her to glue them along the edge of the front of the plate as shown. Have her flip the plate over and glue a claw cutout to each of the two front legs. Encourage her to draw pupils on two white construction paper circles and then glue them to the plate to represent eyes. If desired, display the crabs on a bulletin board and encourage youngsters to add drawings of fish, sea turtles, and other ocean creatures.

Finger Food

You'll see lots of smiling faces when you serve kid-pleasing finger foods for snacktime! Explain that many foods are meant to be eaten without a fork, spoon, or knife. These types of foods are called finger foods. Encourage youngsters to orally count to ten as they hold up their fingers. Next, serve a variety of finger foods, such as cheese, crackers, and finger sandwiches. Then encourage youngsters to use their ten fingers to munch on their snacks.

I Have Ten Fingers

This fingerplay reinforces the concept of the number ten and helps little ones calm their wiggles as they begin circle time.

I have ten fingers,	*Hold up hands.*
And they belong to me.	*Point to yourself.*
I can make them do things.	*Wiggle fingers.*
Would you like to see?	*Continue wiggling fingers.*
I can hold them up high	*Stretch arms over head.*
Or way down low.	*Touch floor with fingers.*
I can make them hide	*Hide hands behind your back.*
And then fold them just so.	*Fold hands in lap.*

Numeral Prints

These kid-pleasing prints are a fun way to make the numeral 10! Use an unsharpened pencil to make an impression of the numeral 10 in a block of floral foam. Use a finger to clean out any excess bits of foam left in the grooves. Invite a youngster to your art center and have her press the foam in a shallow pan of tempera paint. Then help her gently press the foam on a sheet of white construction paper. Encourage her to continue in the same way, covering the paper with prints of the numeral 10. After the paint is dry, encourage her to trace each 10 with her finger and say the word *ten.*

43

Number *12*

Decorating Number 12

These "eggs-tra" special 12s look lovely in a springtime display! Make a white construction paper copy of the 1 and 2 patterns (pages 50 and 51) for each child. Encourage each child to mount the numerals on a sheet of pastel-colored construction paper to make the numeral 12. Next, have each student press his finger on a colorful ink pad and make 12 fingerprints (eggs) on the numeral. Have each youngster use a colorful fine-tip marker to embellish each egg. Then display the finished projects in the classroom. "Egg-cellent"!

A Dozen Doughnuts

It's time to make the doughnuts at this fun center! Place at a table a supply of play dough and a flat box similar to the type baked goods come in. Explain that people often buy doughnuts by the dozen and the word *dozen* means a group of 12 items. Invite children to the table. Encourage them to make play dough doughnuts and then place a dozen in the box. Mmm—doughnuts!

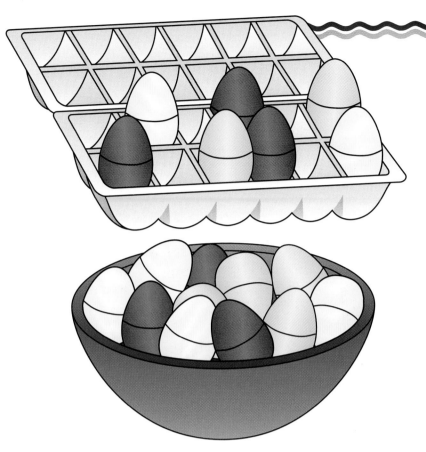

Egg Cartons

Are there 12 eggs in these egg cartons? Youngsters will be the first to let you know with this small-group activity! In advance, clean and sanitize three foam egg cartons. Place plastic eggs in some of the cups in each carton. Then close the cartons and place them at a table along with a supply of extra eggs. Invite three students to the table and explain that they are egg inspectors and their job is to make sure that each carton has a dozen eggs. Give each child a carton. Then have each youngster, in turn, open the carton and count the number of eggs. After she establishes that several eggs are missing, encourage her to place an egg in each available space. Then have her recount the eggs to ensure that there are 12. This carton passes inspection!

Clock Hop

Little ones identify numerals at this center as they hop around a clock! Write a different numeral from 1 to 12 on each of twelve construction paper circles. Use Con-Tact paper to adhere the circles to the floor to resemble a clock as shown. A youngster visits the center and stands on the number 1. Then he hops around the clock, saying the name of each number as he goes. If desired, challenge youngsters by encouraging them to hop on the numbers randomly, naming each number landed on as before.

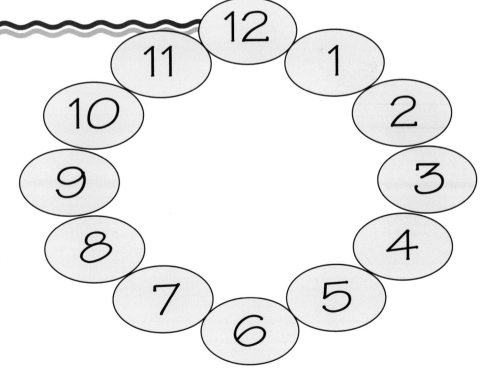

Twelve Months

Youngsters help make a month chart with this timely idea! Write the numerals 1 though 12 on a large sheet of paper and then post the paper in your circle-time area. To begin, ask children to suggest the names of different months; write each month's name next to the appropriate numeral. When youngsters have finished sharing, fill in any remaining spaces. Then have them orally count the number of months on the paper. After establishing that there are 12 months in a year, help students say the names of the months in order.

1. January
2. February
3. March
4. April
5. May
6. June
7. July
8. August
9. September
10. October
11. November
12. December

Hee, hee, hee!

Twelve Little Monkeys

Little ones will go bananas for this rhyme about 12 little monkeys! Gather youngsters in your large-group area. Count 12 students to role-play monkeys and have them sit in a separate group. Lead the children in reciting the rhyme, encouraging the monkeys to add the actions shown. That's some entertaining monkey business!

Twelve little monkeys sitting in a tree.
They were laughing. Hee, hee, hee!   *Hold hand over mouth.*
They were pointing. See, see, see!   *Point up in the air.*
They were clapping. One, two, three!   *Clap hands three times.*

Ticktock

It's time for a counting rhyme! As you lead youngsters in reciting the rhyme, move the large hand of a play clock accordingly.

Ticktock, ticktock—
Move the hands around the clock.
One, two, three, four—
Time to go out the door.
Five, six, seven, eight—
Time for bed; it's getting late.
Nine, ten, eleven, twelve—
Time to bid this rhyme farewell!

Lots of Dots

It's easy to reinforce the concept of the number 12 when you provide little ones with bingo daubers! Write the numeral 12 on a sheet of construction paper. Then make a copy for each child. Have each youngster trace the numeral with her finger and say the word *twelve.* Then encourage her to use a bingo dauber to paint twelve dots on the numeral 12.

Number Parade

Plan a number parade with your youngsters! Divide students into ten groups, with one or more children in each group. Then assign each group a different number from 1 through 10. Use the following ideas to make costumes and props. Then teach the song on page 49 and let the marching begin!

Number 1: Invite a student to carry one large teddy bear. Encourage each remaining student in the group to carry a pennant displaying the numeral 1.

Number 2: Have each youngster carry a poster labeled with the numeral 2 and decorated with pictures of bicycles. In addition, have each child wear a pair of mittens.

Number 3: Have each student carry a colorful triangle cutout labeled with the numeral 3. In addition, encourage each of three youngsters to wear a kitten-ear headband to resemble the three little kittens.

Number 4: Have some youngsters in the group carry toy cars. Encourage the remaining students to carry posters labeled with the numeral 4 and decorated with pictures of four-legged animals.

Number 5: Have each child carry a star wand. To make a star wand, label a star cutout with the numeral 5. Hole-punch each point on the star. Then thread a length of curling ribbon through each hole and tie it in place. Glue the star to a cardboard tube to make a wand.

Number 6: Have each youngster dress up in an insect costume. To make an insect costume, cut a vest from a paper bag. Label the back of the vest with the numeral 6. Then glue three colorful leg cutouts to either side of the vest.

Number 7: Invite each student to carry a days-of-the-week flag. To make a flag, write the numeral 7 on a 12" x 18" sheet of construction paper. Write the days of the week around the numeral. Glue the sheet to a gift wrap tube to make a flag.

Number 8: Have each student carry a construction paper octopus. To make an octopus, staple eight construction paper strips (arms) to a construction paper oval (head). Use a pencil to curl the arms, if desired. Then glue an index card labeled with the numeral 8 to one of the arms.

Number 9: Have each youngster carry his number 9 shaker (see "Number 9 Shakers" on page 36). In addition, invite each child to wear a headband labeled with the numeral 9.

Number 10: Have each child wear a crown made from bulletin board border. Embellish each crown with ten colorful sticky dots. Also invite some students to carry signs labeled with the numeral 10. Encourage other youngsters to wave with all ten fingers.

Number Parade Song

(sung to the tune of "When Johnny Comes Marching Home")

The numbers are marching into town. Hooray! Hooray!
The numbers are marching in a great big number parade.
The ones come first with a teddy bear.
The twos wear mittens, which come in pairs.
Oh, we're so glad the numbers could come today.

The numbers are marching into town. Hooray! Hooray!
The three little kittens march along in this parade.
The fours have four wheels on their toy cars.
The fives hold wands that have lovely stars.
Oh, we're so glad the numbers could come today.

The numbers are marching into town. Hooray! Hooray!
Now insects with six legs are marching on their way.
Here come the sevens—their flags look great!
Then octopi with their legs of eight.
Oh, we're so glad the numbers could come today.

The numbers are marching into town. Hooray! Hooray!
The numbers are marching in a great big number parade.
The nines have shakers filled with nine beans.
And there are ten jewels on each king and queen.
Oh, we're so glad the numbers could come today.

49

Numeral 1 Pattern

Use with "Decorating Number 1" on page 4 and "Decorating Number 12" on page 44.

Mitten Pattern
Use with "Mitten Pairs" on page 8.

Numeral 3 Pattern
Use with "Decorating Number 3" on page 12.

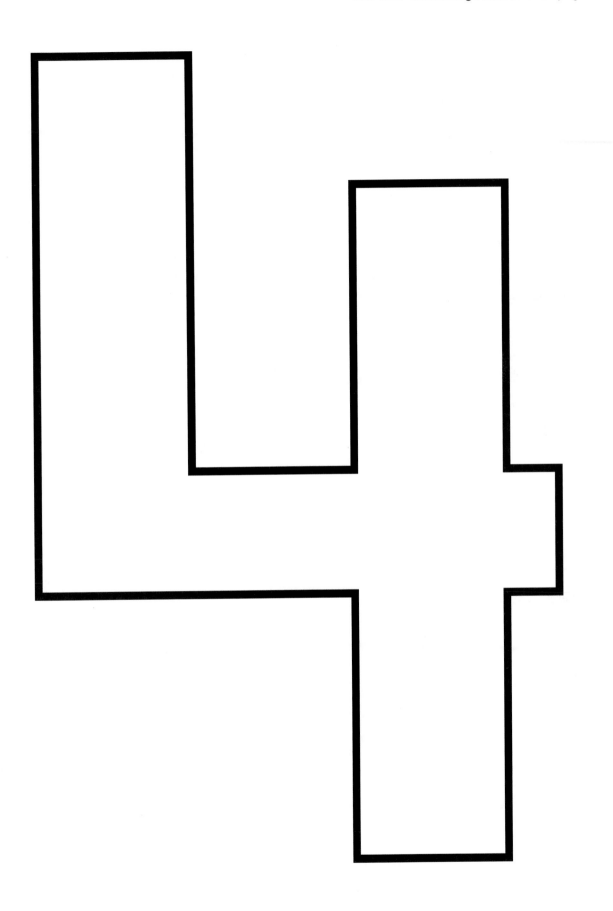

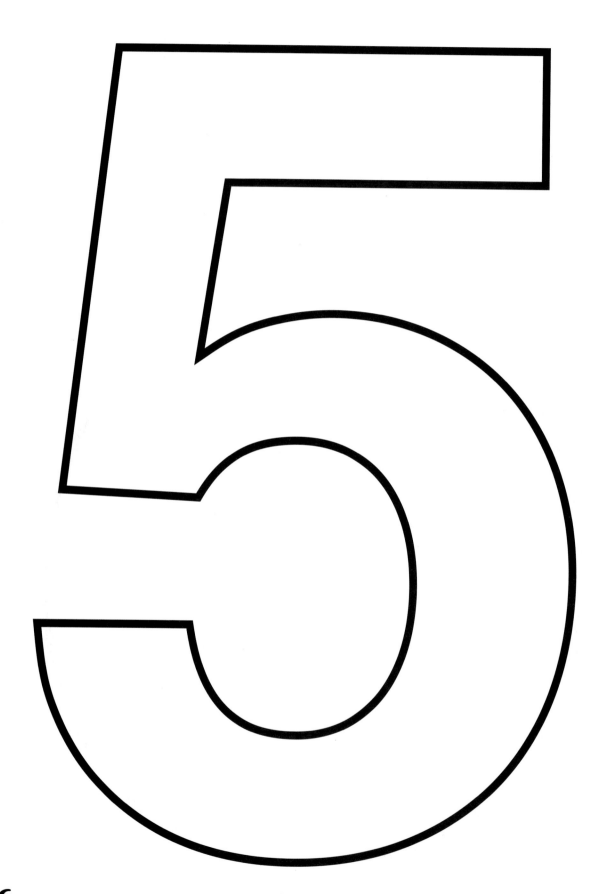

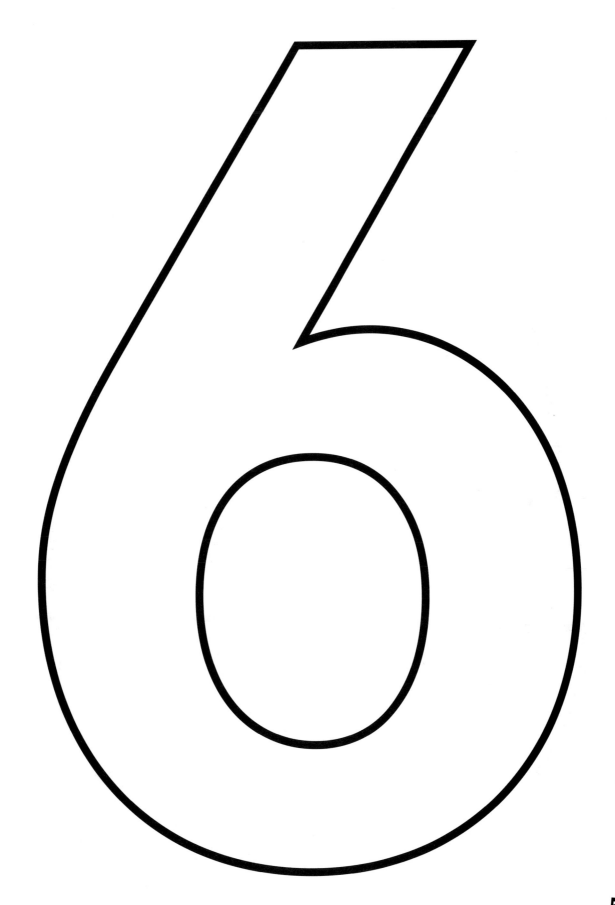

Numeral 7 Pattern

Use with "Decorating Number 7" on page 28.

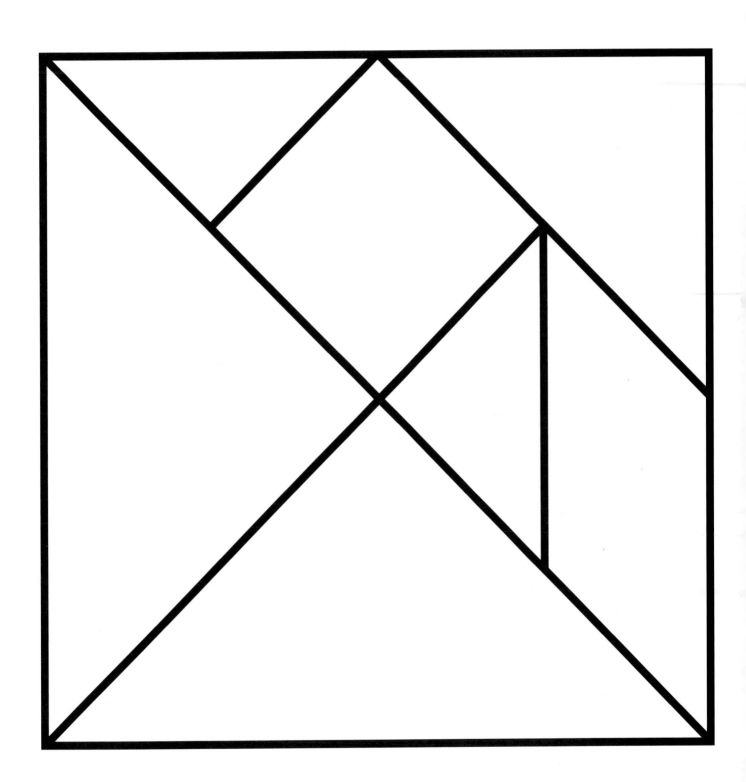

Numeral 8 Pattern
Use with "Decorating Number 8" on page 32.

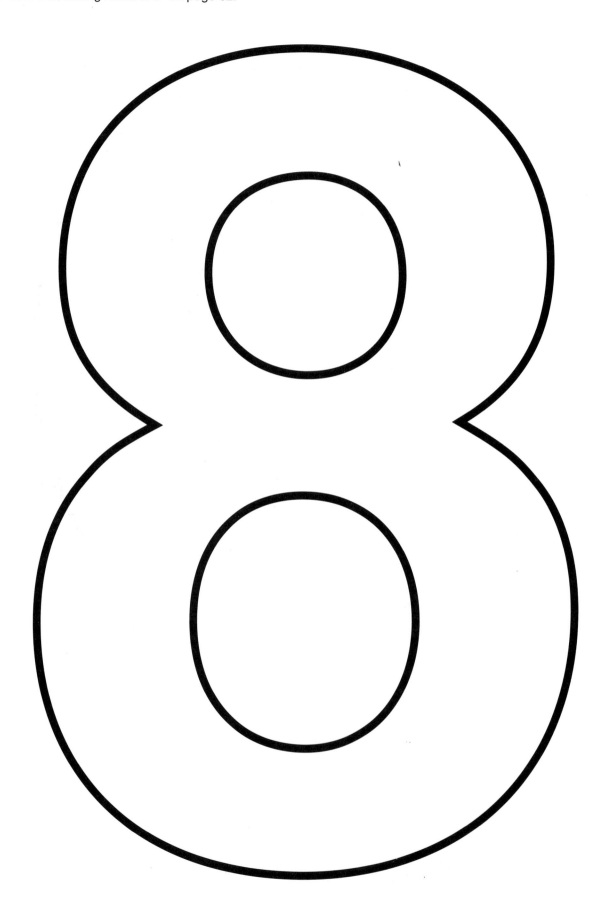

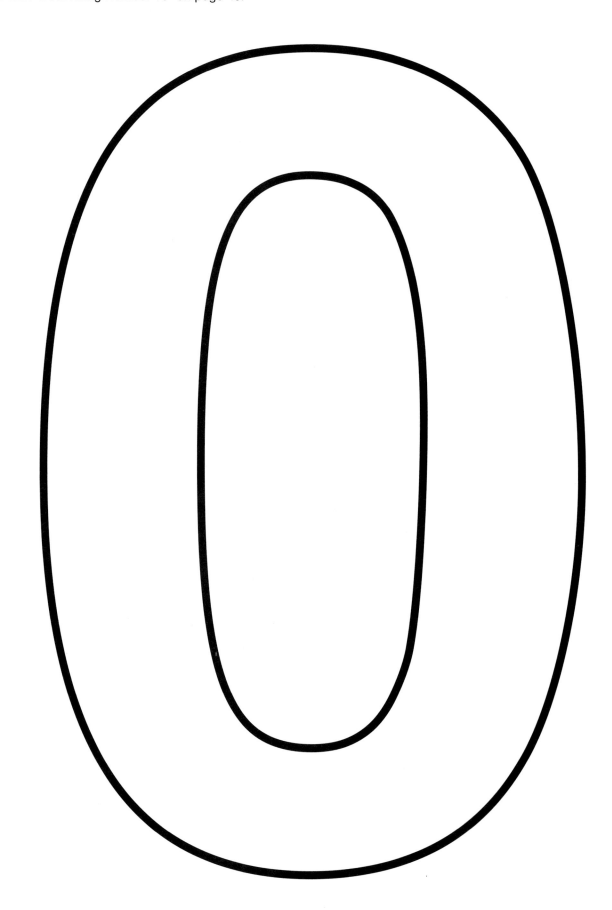

Colors

Red

Red Watermelon

Count on this fruity activity to get a thumbs-up from little ones! In advance, cut a large semicircle from white construction paper for each child. Have each child paint her cutout red and green to resemble a slice of watermelon. Encourage each youngster to identify the color of the edible part of the watermelon. When the paint is dry, help each child make several black thumbprints (seeds) on her watermelon. Then invite each student to share her slice with the class as she counts aloud the number of seeds.

A Basketful of Apples

No doubt this artsy apple-themed activity will be big with your little ones! To prepare, enlarge the apple pattern on page 106. Then make a white construction paper copy for each child. Make a large basket cutout from brown bulletin board paper. Post the paper on a wall in your classroom. To begin, place a dollop of red fingerpaint on each child's apple and have him manipulate the paint until a desired effect is achieved. As he is painting, encourage him to identify the color of the paint. After the paint is dry, help him cut out his apple. Then invite him to glue his apple above the basket. That's a giant bushel of bright red apples!

Ready, Set, Sort!

Youngsters are sure to have lots of fun with these sorting centers! Place a variety of colored items in each of several plastic tubs. Place each tub at a different table. Divide the class into a number of small groups to match the number of tubs. Send one group to each table. Direct each group to sort the objects from their tub into two groups—red and not red. Then, at your signal, have each group place the items back in the tub, mix them up, and then move to a different table. Continue in this manner until each group has sorted each tub. Ready, set, sort!

Stop on Red

Teach students that red means stop with this classroom management idea. Use the pattern on page 106 to make a red construction paper stop sign. Tape a craft stick handle to the sign. To begin, present the stop sign and discuss its color and its meaning. Then use the sign throughout the day to signal students to stop an activity and get ready to begin a new one. Stop—it's time for music!

Seeing Red

Peering through this viewer gives little ones a rosy outlook! Collect a cardboard tube and cut a four-inch square of red cellophane for each child. Have each youngster paint her tube red. When the paint is dry, secure the cellophane around one end with a rubber band as shown. Then invite each child to look through her tube at the surrounding area. Encourage youngsters to describe how objects appear through the tube. Red!

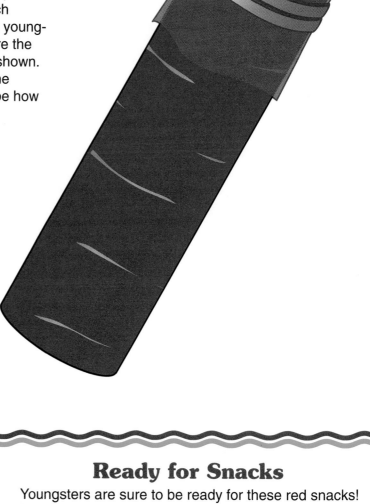

Ready for Snacks

Youngsters are sure to be ready for these red snacks!

- baked red apples
- strawberry slices
- raspberry or cherry gelatin
- cherry pie
- tomato juice

I Love Red

Sing the song below with youngsters. Then encourage each child to name a favorite red object.

(sung to the tune of "Three Blind Mice")

I love red. I love red.
That's what I said. That's what I said.
I love red apples, juicy and sweet.
I love red shoes upon my feet.
I love red cars that zoom down the street.
I love red!

Writing on Red

Ready to write color words? Youngsters will get lots of practice writing the word *red* with this center activity. Make a supply of apple and stop sign patterns (page 106) on red construction paper. Place the patterns and several black markers at a center. Label a red card with the word *red* and post it at the center. A student uses a marker to write the word *red* on an apple and a stop sign. Encourage her to name each letter as she writes. Help her cut out the patterns. Then have her take her writing home to reinforce the color word.

Blue

Blue Bubble Prints

Pop, pop, pop! Youngsters will have a blast blowing bubbles for this print-making activity. Cut a class supply of large white construction paper circles. Add a few squirts of dishwashing liquid to a plastic tub of blue-tinted water. Give each child in a small group a plastic straw and have him practice blowing air out of it. Next, have each child place his straw into the solution and blow until he makes a layer of bubbles. Help each youngster lightly place a circle on the bubbles to make a print. Lay the circles flat to dry. Repeat the activity with each small group of students. Display the bubble prints on a bulletin board titled "Bubblin' Up Blue!"

Bluebird Puppet

Your little ones will enjoy making this sweet little bluebird! Make an enlarged blue construction paper copy of the bluebird pattern (page 107) for each child. Cut out the patterns. Place the cutouts at a table along with bowls of glue, paintbrushes, and a supply of small blue craft feathers. Invite each child in a small group to brush glue onto her bluebird and then press several feathers in the glue. Lay the bluebirds flat to dry. Then help each child tape a personalized craft stick onto the back of the bluebird to make a puppet. Encourage children to use their puppets as props as they sing the song on page 71.

Blueberry Toss

Everyone is a blue-ribbon player with this fun hand-eye coordination game. Make a blue construction paper copy of the ribbon pattern on page 107 for each child. To prepare, set a small basket on the floor and then attach a strip of tape several feet away. Give each player ten blue pom-poms to represent blueberries. Ask him to stand behind the tape line. Then have him try to toss one blueberry at a time into the basket. Have each child count the number of blueberries in his basket. Award each player a personalized blue ribbon for his effort. Then have him identify the color of his award. Blue!

Shades of Blue

Little ones will love this colorful sorting activity! From a paint supply store, gather matching pairs of paint sample strips in different shades of blue. Mix up the strips and place them at a center. Have each child sort the strips into pairs of matching shades of blue. Then have her mix up the strips for the next center visitor. Sky blue is the best!

Blue Sky, Blue Water

Does it fly or swim? Youngsters' thinking skills will be challenged when they classify a collection of creatures. Cut a large piece of blue felt and place it on a flannelboard. Attach a length of yarn or masking tape across the middle of the felt to divide it into two sections to represent sky and water. Cut a class supply of magazine pictures of animals that fly or swim. Laminate the pictures for durability, prepare the pictures for flannelboard use, and place the pictures in a plastic tub. Invite a child to choose an animal and decide whether it usually swims or flies. Then help her attach the picture to the corresponding section of felt. Continue until each child has had a turn. If desired, place this activity at a center for each child to enjoy.

Berry Blue Snacks

Youngsters are sure to be "berry" happy with these blue snacks!

- blueberries
- blueberry pancakes
- blueberry muffins
- blue yogurt
- blue fruit drink
- blue-tinted frosting on graham crackers

70

I Love Blue

Sing the song below with youngsters. Then encourage each child to name a favorite blue object.

(sung to the tune of "Three Blind Mice")

I love blue. I love blue.
Yes, I do. Yes, I do.
I love to fly way up high,
Up into the big blue sky,
Over blue water—my, oh my!
I love blue.

Blue Prints

Blue stars, blue triangles, and blue circles! Little ones label all the cutouts at this center with the word *blue*. Cut several different shades of blue construction paper into various shapes. Place the shapes and several different shades of blue crayons and markers at a center. Label a card with the word *blue* and post it at the center. Have each child choose several shapes. Next, have her use a different crayon or marker to write the word *blue* on each shape. Encourage her to name each letter as she writes the word.

Green

Tinted Turtles

This shiny turtle puppet will make a splash with your little ones. Use the patterns on page 108 to make a green construction paper turtle for each child. Cut a supply of one-inch squares from two different shades of green cellophane. Give each child a pattern and a handful of squares. Prompt her to identify the color of her materials. Then have her count her squares before gluing them onto the turtle shell. When the glue is dry, tape a personalized craft stick onto the back to make a puppet for each child. Then lead your little ones and their puppets on a turtle stroll around the classroom.

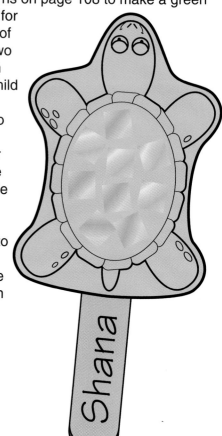

Leafy Lineup

Youngsters will line up to pick a leaf from this tree! Gather several large green leaves. Remove the wrappers from several different shades of green crayons. To begin, model for students how to make a leaf rubbing on drawing paper. Have each child make his own leaf rubbing. Then help each youngster cut out his leaf and write his name on the back. Attach all the leaves to a classroom tree display. Each day, have a different student pick a leaf from the tree. Prompt him to identify the name on the back to determine the daily line leader. Today's leader is Derek!

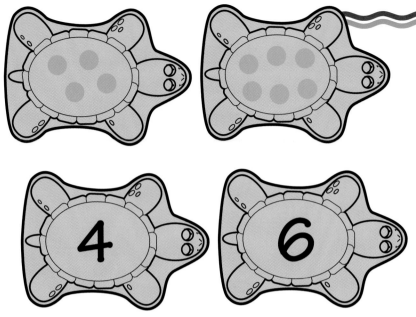

Spotted Turtles

Spot these green turtles helping youngsters practice counting and number recognition skills! Make twelve green construction paper copies of the turtle pattern on page 108. Cut out the turtles. Place one to six green sticker dots on each of six turtles, making sure each turtle has a different number of dots. Program each of the remaining turtles with a matching numeral. Laminate the turtles for durability and place them at a center. A child counts the spots on a turtle and then matches it to the turtle with the corresponding numeral. He continues in the same manner until all the remaining turtles are matched.

Hoppin' Green

Hop, hop, hop! Your little froglets will jump for joy with this musical activity. Use the pattern on page 109 to make five green lily pad cutouts. Also make several lily pads in different colors. Use Con-Tact paper to adhere the lily pads to the floor in a random fashion. To begin, invite a group of up to five students to the area and have them form a circle around the lily pads. Play music as youngsters hop around the circle. Periodically stop the music and encourage each child to stand on a green lily pad and croak like a frog. After each child has found a green lily pad, resume playing the music and have youngsters continue as before. Your little hoppers are sure to request several rounds of this fun game!

Ribbit!

Green Mix-up

Which two colors mix to make green? Little ones find out when you introduce secondary colors with this vivid mixing activity. Partially fill a clear plastic cup with water and set it in students' view. Have your youngsters sit in a circle around the cup. Invite two students to simultaneously place drops of yellow and blue food coloring into the cup. Encourage youngsters to observe the water and describe what they see. Explain that mixing two primary colors, blue and yellow, creates a secondary color, green. If desired, repeat the activity using different combinations of primary colors to make other secondary colors. Lovely!

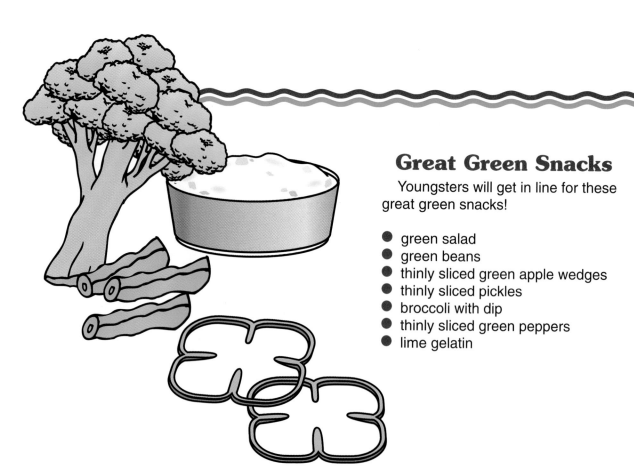

Great Green Snacks

Youngsters will get in line for these great green snacks!

- green salad
- green beans
- thinly sliced green apple wedges
- thinly sliced pickles
- broccoli with dip
- thinly sliced green peppers
- lime gelatin

I Love Green

Sing the song below with youngsters. Then encourage each child to name a favorite green object.

(sung to the tune of "Three Blind Mice")

I love green. I love green.
It's so keen. It's so keen.
I love green grapes and crisp green beans.
My lucky shirt is the color green.
It's simply the best color that I've seen.
I love green!

Green Frog, Green Frog

Youngsters will be croakin' about this green-seeking language game! Gather students in a circle and choose one child to be the green frog. Have the green frog sit in the center of the circle. Lead youngsters in reciting the rhyme shown. Have the green frog describe one green object he sees in the classroom. Then have youngsters take turns guessing the name of the object. The child that guesses correctly trades places with the green frog. Continue playing in the same way, inviting a different child to be the green frog for each new round.

Green frog, green frog,
Up in a tree,
What green things
Do you see?

Yellow

Yellow Daffodils

Your classroom will be in full bloom when youngsters help make this flowery display. For each student, make a white construction paper copy of the flower pattern on page 112. Have each child paint her flower yellow. Allow time for the paint to dry. Then help each youngster cut out her flower. Next, have her glue a mini cupcake liner to the middle of the flower. Encourage her to cut leaves and a stem from green construction paper and glue them to the flower. Then display the finished flowers on a bulletin board.

Sunshine Puppet

Youngsters will enjoy making these sunny puppets! Enlarge a copy of the sun pattern (page 110). Then make a yellow construction paper copy for each child. Cut out the patterns. Encourage each child to glue a variety of yellow craft items to the sun, such as pom-poms, yarn, and tissue paper scraps. Next, have him use yellow glitter glue to give his sunshine a smiling face. When the glue is dry, attach a personalized jumbo craft stick to the back of each child's sunshine to make a puppet. It's a sunshine day!

Ducks on a Pond

These fuzzy yellow ducks are all in a row! Make three yellow construction paper copies of the duck pattern on page 110 for each child. Cut out the patterns. Have each youngster glue a small yellow craft feather onto each of his ducks. Then help him trim a 9" x 12" sheet of blue construction paper to resemble a pond. Have each child glue his ducks in a row onto his pond. Then encourage each student to touch each duck as he names its color. Yellow! Yellow! Yellow!

Ducks in a Row

All your little ducklings will be quacking over this size sequencing activity. Use the pattern on page 110 to make five yellow duck cutouts in different sizes. Laminate the ducks for durability. Invite a child to spread the ducks out on a table to observe the different sizes. Then have him sequence the ducks from smallest to largest. Quack, quack, quack!

Y Is for Yellow

Yum, yum! Bake up a cake to reinforce the beginning letter of the color word *yellow*. Have youngsters help stir up a yellow cake mix according to the package directions. Pour the cake into a rectangular pan and bake. When the cake is cool, cut it in half lengthwise. Then cut one section to make a point as shown. Cut the remaining section in half. Carefully remove the sections from the pan. Eat or discard the two small triangles. Position the remaining sections in a Y formation on a sheet of cardboard lined with aluminum foil. Use yellow frosting to cover the cake. Show students the cake and ask them to name the letter. Then explain that the word *yellow* begins with the letter *Y*. Finally, give each child a slice of yummy yellow cake!

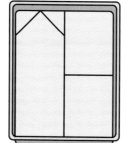

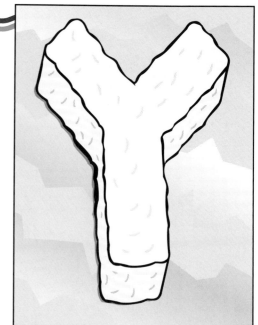

Dramatic Play

Reinforce the color yellow with the following dramatic-play props:

- yellow plastic dishes
- plastic bananas and lemons
- empty lemon pudding packages
- yellow silk flowers
- yellow rain hats and coats
- yellow rain boots

Yummy Yellow Snacks

Youngsters are sure to say yes to these yummy yellow snacks!

- banana slices
- banana pudding
- pineapple slices
- thinly sliced yellow apple wedges
- corn on the cob with butter
- lemon meringue pie
- yellow crackers

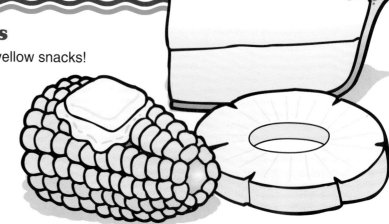

I Love Yellow

Sing the song shown with youngsters. Then encourage each child to name a favorite yellow object.

(sung to the tune of "Three Blind Mice")

I love yellow. I love yellow.
It's so mellow. It's so mellow.
I love yellow flowers that grow to the sky.
I love yellow ducks that swim right by.
I love yellow slickers that keep me dry.
I love yellow!

My Yellow Book

Youngsters will be so proud when they make these little yellow booklets. For each child, make a blank four-page booklet with a yellow cover. Provide access to a supply of magazines. To begin, ask youngsters to name objects that are yellow as you record their ideas on a sheet of chart paper. Then give each child a booklet and crayons. Have her draw a picture or glue a magazine picture of a yellow object on each page of her booklet. Then help her label each page with the pictured object's name. Encourage her to write her name and the title shown on the booklet cover, providing assistance as needed. Invite students to read their booklets to their classmates. Then send the booklets home for students to share with their families.

My Yellow Book by Sandy

yellow bus

Orange

Pleasingly Orange Pumpkins

Here's a pleasing way to make an orange pumpkin! Enlarge the pumpkin pattern on page 111. Then make a white construction paper copy of the pattern for each child. Cut small squares of different shades of orange crepe paper. Set the pumpkins and squares at a table along with a supply of glue and paintbrushes. Invite a small group of students to the table and have each child brush glue on a pumpkin. Next, have him cover his pumpkin with crepe paper squares. Encourage each student to identify the color of the squares. After the glue dries, invite each child to take his pumpkin home to share with his family.

Goldfish Bowl

No water is needed to make this orange fish puppet swim! Give each child a paper plate with a slit cut in the bottom, as shown, and have her color it blue. Cut a circle from the center of a second plate; then invert it and staple it atop the colored plate to resemble a fishbowl. Next, give each youngster a fish pattern (page 111) and have her color it orange. Then help her cut it out and tape a craft stick to the back of it to make a puppet. Help her insert her fish puppet into the slit to make it swim in the fishbowl. Encourage each child to use her puppet to perform the rhyme in "Goldfish, Goldfish" on page 83.

Where's the Orange?

In this small-group activity, youngsters practice positional words with a bunch of oranges! To prepare, make six felt oranges. Cut a large felt bowl. Gather a group of six children around your flannelboard. Place the bowl on the flannelboard and give each youngster an orange. Encourage students to identify the color of their oranges. Next, have one child at a time place his orange in a specific location on the flannelboard, using positional words such as *above, below, on,* and *beside.* Continue the activity by encouraging each child to remove a specific orange.

Counting Goldfish

Little orange fish frolic in the sea with this tasty counting center. In advance, label each of six blue plastic plates with a different numeral from 1 to 6. Prepare a resealable plastic bag of 21 cheddar-flavored Goldfish crackers. Then place the plates and crackers at a center. Have a youngster identify the color of the crackers. Encourage her to name the numeral on each plate and then place the corresponding number of crackers on the plate. After checking the child's work, give her some fresh fishies to munch on!

Making Orange

What makes orange? Youngsters discover the answer with this colorful investigation. Gather a small group of students and show them red, yellow, and blue play dough. Ask youngsters to guess which two colors mixed together will make orange. Have each student test her guess by squishing together two different colors of play dough. Encourage each child to share the results of her experiment with the class. I made orange!

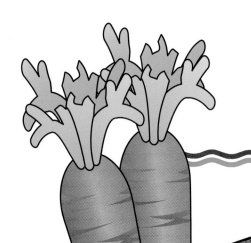

Orange All Around

Help students identify the color orange with these zesty additions to your dramatic-play center.

- plastic oranges
- plastic carrots
- orange plastic bowls and cups
- empty orange gelatin boxes
- orange scarves
- orange hats

Oh-So-Orange Snacks

Serve one of the orange snacks listed below in an orange plastic bowl or cup. What a fun serving suggestion!

- orange juice
- orange slices
- orange gelatin
- orange crackers
- pumpkin pie

82

I Love Orange

Sing the song below with youngsters. Then encourage each child to name a favorite orange object.

(sung to the tune of "Three Blind Mice")

I love orange. I love orange.
It's so bright. It's so bright.
I love orange pumpkins that grow in the fall.
I love orange goldfish so cute and small.
I love my great big orange beach ball.
I love orange.

Goldfish, Goldfish

Teach youngsters the rhyme shown. Then encourage them to use their puppets from "Goldfish Bowl" on page 80 to make up movements to go along with the words.

Goldfish, goldfish, swim around.
Goldfish, goldfish, up and down.
Goldfish, goldfish, fast and slow.
Goldfish, goldfish, around you go!

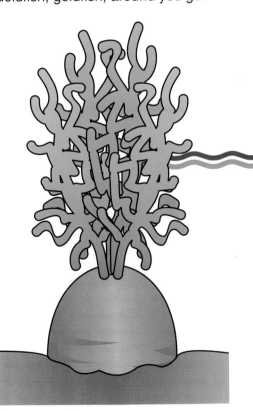

I'm a Little Carrot

Share the story *The Carrot Seed* by Ruth Krauss with youngsters and then teach them the song below. Guide each child to perform actions as you sing the song.

(sung to the tune of "I'm a Little Teapot")

I'm a little carrot, orange and green.
I grow in the ground where my orange can't be seen.
When I get big, I'll give a shout.
"Please come over and pull me out!"

Purple

Purple Posies

These lovely purple posies will look radiant on a bulletin board in your classroom! Use the pattern on page 112 to make a large dark purple flower cutout and a small light purple flower cutout for each child. Encourage each student to identify the color of the cutouts. Then invite her to glue the large cutout to a 9" x 12" sheet of construction paper, leaving the petals unattached. Have her glue the small cutout on top of the large one to resemble a flower. Then encourage her to bend the tips of both sets of petals to create a three-dimensional effect as shown. If desired, have each child glue a crumpled ball of purple tissue paper to the center of the flower. Then invite her to use a marker to add a stem and leaves. Attach the finished flowers to a bulletin board titled "Purple Posies."

Purple Grapes

Making this cluster of grapes gives youngsters practice with color recognition and counting. In advance, gather several purple bingo daubers. Give each child in a small group a sheet of construction paper and help her make a row of five purple dots, as shown. Guide her to make a row of four purple dots centered below the first row. Then help her make three more rows of dots, each row having one less dot than the previous one to resemble a cluster of grapes. When the ink is dry, have her draw green leaves and a vine around her grapes. What color are the grapes? Purple!

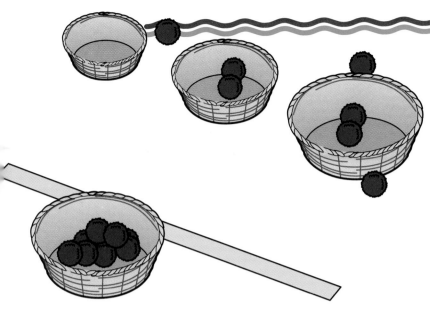

Plum Tossin'

This fun activity helps develop youngsters' hand-eye coordination skills. Gather several large purple pom-poms. Also gather three different-size baskets plus one extra basket. Place the pom-poms in the extra basket and space the remaining baskets in a row on the floor. Place a tape line on the floor several feet away from the row of baskets. Invite a small group of youngsters to line up behind the tape line. Give each child three pom-poms and tell her they represent plums. Ask her to identify the color of the plums. Invite her to toss the plums into any of the baskets. After each child has had a turn, collect the pom-poms and invite the group to play another round of Plum Tossin'.

Grape Puzzle

Practice problem-solving skills with this grape center activity. Use a purple marker to program five large craft sticks with rows of dots to resemble grapes as shown. Show youngsters the completed puzzle and help them count the number of grapes in each row. Point out that the number of grapes is one less with each successive row. Then mix up the sticks and place them at a center. Invite one child at a time to complete the puzzle and then count the grapes.

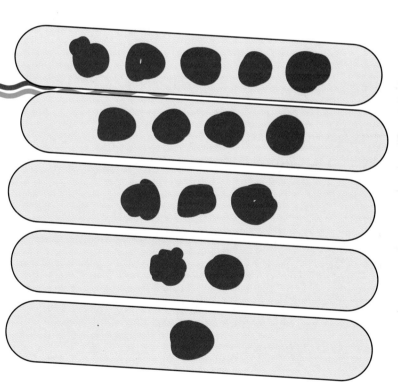

Discovering Purple Flowers

This investigation is a flowery way to remember the color purple. Bring a collection of real or artificial purple flowers to school. Gather youngsters and let them observe the collection of flowers. Encourage them to identify things that are the same about the flowers and things that are different. Discuss the different shades of purple in the flower collection. Then place the flowers at a center for further investigation.

Purple Play

Add purple power to your dramatic-play area!

- plastic purple grapes
- plastic purple cups and plates
- purple napkins
- purple scarves
- purple shirts
- purple visors or hats
- a purple feather boa
- purple plastic sunglasses
- purple gloves

Purple Snacks

These are pleasing purple snacks!

- purple grape juice
- grape gelatin
- grape milk shakes (blend grape juice and vanilla ice cream)
- grape-flavored drink

I Love Purple

Lead youngsters in singing the song below. Then encourage each child to name a favorite purple object.

(sung to the tune of "Three Blind Mice")

I love purple. I love purple.
Yes I do. Yes I do.
I love purple plums that grow on trees.
I love purple violets, so fancy.
I love purple butterflies that fly by me.
I love purple.

Purple Cow Puppet

This cute cow puppet will help youngsters recognize the color purple. Make a purple construction paper copy of the cow pattern on page 112 for each child. Cut out the cows and help each student attach a personalized craft stick to the back of his cow to make a puppet. Gather youngsters and ask them to identify the color of their cows. Ask them to think of different ways that a cow might become purple and record their ideas on a sheet of chart paper. Then teach students the poem "The Purple Cow" by Gelett Burgess. Have youngsters perform the poem with their purple cows. Moo!

Brown

Fuzzy Wuzzy Bears

Fuzzy Wuzzy was a bear puppet! Make a brown construction paper copy of the bear pattern on page 113 for each child. Cut a small brown felt oval for each student. Show youngsters one of the ovals and ask them to identify its color. Have each child draw any desired features on the bear and then glue the felt oval to its tummy. Help her tape a personalized craft stick to the back of the bear to make a puppet. Then have your little ones use their puppets to perform a favorite teddy bear rhyme.

Brown Vest

A simple brown paper grocery bag makes dress-up fun! In advance, cut a brown paper bag into a vest for each child. Gather youngsters and write the word *brown* on a sheet of chart paper. Have them identify the color word. Encourage students to name brown objects as you record their ideas on the paper. Give each child a vest and markers. Help each youngster write the word *brown* on his vest. Then have him draw pictures of brown objects on his vest, using the chart paper as a reference if needed. Encourage each child to label his drawings. Then invite each student to show off his vest in a classroom fashion show!

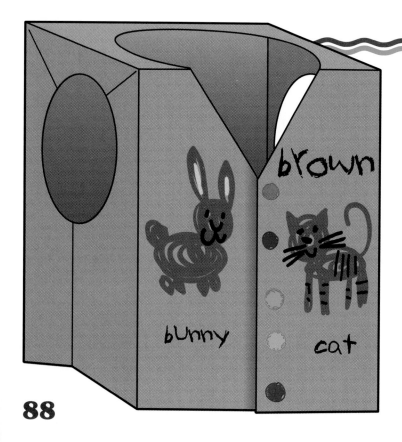

Turkey Greeting

Gobble, gobble! This little brown turkey makes a festive greeting card. Give each child a white construction paper copy of the turkey pattern on page 113. Encourage each student to color her turkey brown. Then have her cut out the turkey and glue it to the front of a brown construction paper card, leaving the top portion unattached. Next, encourage each child to dip the bottom of each of several craft feathers in glue and insert them behind the cutout as shown. Let the glue dry. Then have each student personalize her card to give to a loved one.

Football Toss

Watch your little football fans toss around the color word *brown!* To prepare, use markers to draw a football goalpost on a brown box and place it against a wall. Tape a line several feet in front of the box. Write the word *brown* on a sheet of chart paper. Then post the paper nearby for youngsters to use as a reference. Have a small group of up to five students line up behind the tape. Give the first child in line a small plastic football and have him attempt to toss the ball into the box. If the ball goes in, encourage him to use a brown crayon to write the first letter in the word *brown* on the chart paper, using the word as a reference if needed. Proceed in the same manner, having each child toss the football and write the next letter in the word each time he gets the ball in the box. Play is finished when youngsters have written all five letters.

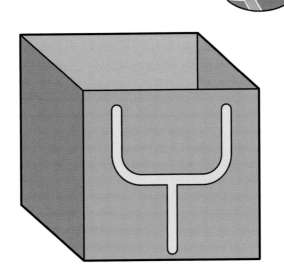

Dramatic Play

Reinforce the color brown by adding several brown objects to your dramatic-play area.

- brown wooden bowls and spoons
- brown boots
- brown belts
- brown hats
- empty chocolate pudding packages
- clean chocolate milk containers

Brown Snacks

Serve up some yummy brown snacks!

- chocolate brownies
- gingerbread cookies
- cinnamon-sugar toast
- whole wheat rolls
- root beer
- chocolate cupcakes
- chocolate pudding

I Love Brown

Sing the song below with youngsters. Then encourage each child to name a favorite brown object.

(sung to the tune of "Three Blind Mice")

I love brown. I love brown.
It's all around. It's all around.
I love brown on my teddy bear.
I love brown shoes—I have 20 pairs.
I love brown dirt everywhere.
I love brown.

Let's Look for Brown

Lead youngsters in singing the song below. Have students look for and then name brown objects in the classroom.

(sung to the tune of "The Farmer in the Dell")

Oh, let's look for brown.
I know it can be found.
Heigh-ho, here we go.
Oh, let's look for brown.

Muddy Writing

Little ones will be happy to play in the mud for this word activity. Give each child in a small group a foam plate with a scoop of chocolate pudding to represent mud. Show students a large card labeled with the color word *brown*. Have them say the word and spell it out loud. Next, invite each child to use two fingers to spread out the mud on his plate. Then have him use one finger to write the word *brown* in his mud. Encourage him to name each letter as he writes the word. Then have little ones lick those messy fingers!

91

Black

Black Tracks

Youngsters will make tracks to this fun painting center! Set out a shallow tray of black tempera paint and several different toy cars or trucks. Gather a small group of students and have them identify the color of the paint. Then give each child at the center a large sheet of paper. Invite each youngster to roll a car in the paint and then roll it onto her paper until a desired effect is achieved. Vroom!

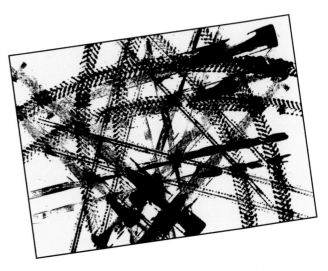

Animals at Nighttime

Which animals come out at nighttime? Your youngsters will be eager to share their answers to this question to make a nifty nighttime scene! Encourage students to name animals that come out at night as you write each name on a sheet of chart paper. Then have each child use crayons to draw a picture of nighttime animals on a sheet of white construction paper, using the list as a guide if needed. Ask him to leave the sky white, but urge him to add a moon and stars. Finally, have each student brush black watercolor paint across his entire picture to enhance the nighttime scene!

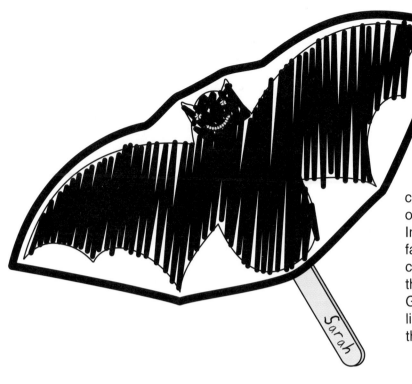

Black Bat Puppets

Black bats will be swooping around your classroom with these fun puppets! Make a copy of the bat pattern on page 114 for each child. Invite each child to color her bat black and add facial features with glitter glue. Then help her cut it out. Attach a personalized craft stick to the back of each child's bat to make a puppet. Give each youngster her bat. Then dim the lights in your classroom and have students "fly" their bats while they recite bat-themed rhymes!

Five Black Cats

Calling all kitties! This catchy rhyme gives youngsters practice with color words and counting. Cut out five black felt cats using the cat pattern on page 114 as a guide. Place the cats on a flannelboard. Copy the rhyme below on a sheet of chart paper. Ask students to name the color of the cats on the flannelboard and then count them out loud. Then read the rhyme to youngsters, removing each cat from the flannelboard when indicated. Repeat the activity several times; then place the flannelboard and chart paper at a center for further practice.

Five black cats meowed at the door.
One went inside, and then there were four.

Four black cats climbed up a tree.
One went home, and then there were three.

Three black cats had nothing to do.
One went home, and then there were two.

Two black cats played in the sun.
One went home, and then there was one.

One black cat all alone had no fun.
So he went home, and then there were none!

Colorful Memory

Exercise youngsters' memories with this small-group color-recognition game. In advance, place a selection of familiar objects on a tray, including several black items. Gather a small group of students and review the color black. Then present the tray of objects. Have youngsters observe the tray for one minute. Then remove it from their view. Encourage children to recall the black objects. List their responses on the board. Then reveal the tray so that youngsters can check their answers.

black sheep

Black Animals
by Ms. Hansen's Class

Black Animals Book

Help youngsters create this animal-themed class book to review the color word *black.* Ask youngsters to name animals that have black fur, skin, or feathers, such as cats, bats, or crows. Record their ideas on a sheet of chart paper. Next, have each child choose a favorite animal from the list. Help her write the word *black* and the animal's name at the bottom of a sheet of paper as shown. Then have her draw a picture of the chosen animal. When each child is finished, bind the pages together with a cover titled "Black Animals." Place the book at a center for all to read and enjoy.

Black Snacks

Serve one of these special treats on a black napkin.

- Oreo cookies
- cupcakes with black frosting
- sliced black olives

94

I Love Black

Lead youngsters in singing the song below. Then encourage each child to name a favorite black object.

(sung to the tune of "Three Blind Mice")

I love black. I love black.
Yes, I do. How about you?
I love the black sky I see at night.
I love black panthers with eyes so bright.
I love black licorice; it tastes just right.
I love black.

Yackin' Black

Youngsters will be yacking about rhyming words with this activity. In advance, cut a large crayon shape from black poster board. Then show students the crayon cutout and ask them to name its color. Help youngsters list words that rhyme with *black*. Use white chalk to write each rhyming word on the crayon cutout. Then have students help read the list.

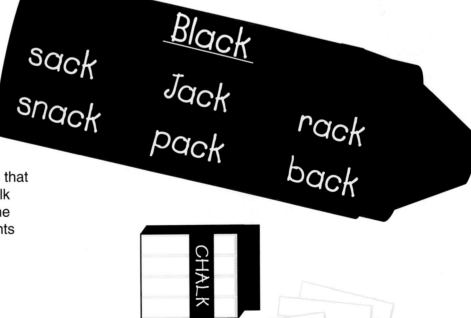

Black
sack
snack
Jack
pack
rack
back

CHALK

Glittering Snowpals

These glistening white snowpals will add sparkle to any display! Make a white construction paper copy of the snowpal pattern on page 115 for each child. Have each child color her snowpal's hat and then add facial features and any other desired decorations. Help each youngster cut out her snowpal. Next, have her brush thinned glue onto her snowpal. Then direct her to place it in a shallow box and sprinkle white glitter over the glue. Shake off the excess glitter and lay the snowpal flat to dry. Later, display all the snowpals on a snowy seasonal bulletin board.

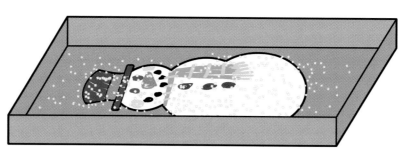

cloudy white rabbit

Cloudy White

Inspire youngsters' creativity with some quick cloud watching and a puffy project! If possible, take students outside to observe the clouds. Encourage each child to identify the color of the clouds. Then have him use his imagination to describe their shapes. After returning to the classroom, give each child a sheet of light blue construction paper and a handful of cotton batting. Encourage each child to use the batting to re-create a cloud shape he observed. Then help him glue it in place on his paper. If desired, help each child label his cloud creation.

Four White Bunnies

Hop into color word skills with this flannelboard activity! Make four white felt bunnies, using the pattern on page 115 as a guide. Write the provided rhyme on a large sheet of chart paper. Place one bunny on the flannelboard and ask youngsters to name its color. Next, point to the word *white* in the rhyme as youngsters repeat the word. Then recite the rhyme with youngsters, adding each bunny to the flannelboard when indicated. When youngsters are comfortable with the activity, place the flannelboard and chart paper at a center for independent practice.

One white bunny had nothing to do.
Along came a friend; then there were two.

Two white bunnies were playing happily.
Another stopped by; then there were three.

Three white bunnies were wishing for one more.
Their wish came true; then there were four.

Four white bunnies were having lots of fun.
They all hopped away; now there are none!

Where Is the Snowflake?

Little white snowflakes help youngsters practice positional words. To prepare, make a class supply of white construction paper snowflakes and laminate them for durability. Have students sit in a circle; then give each child a snowflake. Encourage students to identify the color of the snowflakes. Then have youngsters listen carefully as you give them a direction that uses a positional word, such as "Place the snowflake *beside* your ear." Encourage students to follow the direction. Continue in the same way with different positional words. Put the snowflake *on* your head!

Winter Whiteout

Spotlight the color white with a quick lesson in animal camouflage. In advance, make or gather several pictures of white animals, such as snowy owls, snowshoe hares, polar bears, or Arctic foxes. Prepare a white bulletin board with white construction paper snowdrifts, snowflakes, and clouds. Attach the animal pictures to the board. Gather students and ask them to name the white objects. Next, ask them to think of reasons why it is helpful for animals that live in snowy areas to be white. Explain that the animals' white color makes it difficult to see them in white snow, so they are protected from other animals and people. Encourage students to draw pictures of white animals and attach them to the bulletin board. Now where did that polar bear go?

Wonderful White Snacks

These white snacks are full of flavor!

- milk
- vanilla cupcakes with white icing
- cream cheese on bagels
- white bread
- instant mashed potatoes

I Love White

Sing the song below with youngsters. Then encourage each child to name a favorite white object.

(sung to the tune of "Three Blind Mice")

I love white. I love white.
That is right; I love white.
I love white snowflakes that fall from the sky.
I love white bunnies so soft and shy.
I love white clouds as they float by.
I love white.

Keep Brushing

Promote dental care when youngsters pretend to brush their teeth as they sing this toothy song.

(sung to the tune of "Are You Sleeping")

Brushing up, brushing down.
All around, all around.
Keep your smile bright.
Keep your teeth white.
Brushing up, brushing down.

Riddling White

Get little ones thinking about the color white with these riddles. Before sharing the following riddles with youngsters, give them a hint as to the answers—they are all white objects!

What form many shapes and float in the sky? *(clouds)*
What are soft, sweet, and taste great in hot chocolate? *(marshmallows)*
What is a liquid that you pour on cereal? *(milk)*
What brown-skinned vegetable is white on the inside and tastes great mashed or fried? *(potato)*
What is cold and falls from the sky in the wintertime? *(snow)*

99

Piggy Puppet

Use this cute piggy puppet to practice counting skills. Make a white construction paper copy of the pig pattern on page 116 for each child. Have each youngster paint her pattern pink. When the paint is dry, help her cut out her pig. Have her use markers to draw a face on the cutout. Then attach a personalized craft stick onto the back of each child's pig. Invite youngsters to use the resulting puppets when they perform the counting song on page 103.

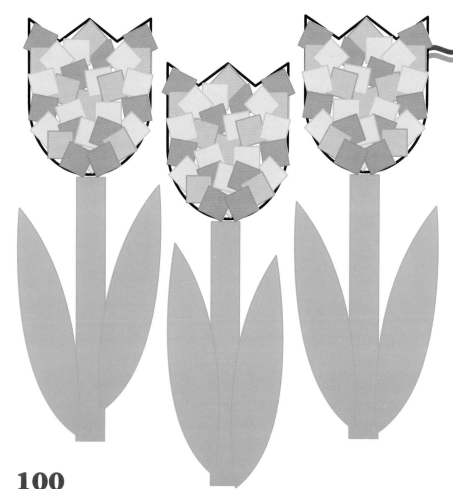

Pink-Tinted Tulips

Set the tone for learning the color pink with these pink posies. Enlarge a copy of the tulip pattern on page 116. Then make a white construction paper copy for each child. Cut out the patterns. Encourage each child to spread glue onto her flower and then cover it with torn tissue paper pieces in several shades of pink. Allow time for the glue to dry. Then display the flowers on a bulletin board with construction paper stems and leaves.

Pink

Pink Search

Little ones will love this "color-rific" circle-time idea! Make a class supply of pink cutouts. Before youngsters arrive for the day, hide each pink cutout in the classroom. At circle time, invite each student to search for one pink cutout. When each youngster finds a cutout, have him bring it back to your circle-time area. Then have him tape his cutout to a sheet of chart paper labeled with the word *pink.*

Lacing Pigs

These little pink piggies provide lots of fine-motor practice! To prepare, make four large pig cutouts from pink poster board, using the pattern on page 116 as a guide. Laminate the pig cutouts for durability. Then punch holes along the outer edge of each pig. Tie an appropriate length of pink yarn to each pig. Then wrap tape around the free end of the yarn. Place the pigs in a center. Invite up to four children to visit the center and have each child lace a pig. Oink! Oink!

Pink Mix

What two colors make pink? Youngsters will be eager to find out with this discovery activity. Place red, yellow, blue, and white paint at your art table. Invite a small group of children to the table and give each child a paper plate and several cotton swabs. Place on each child's plate a spoonful of each paint color. Have each youngster use the cotton swabs to mix pairs of colors, searching for the combination that makes pink. When each child discovers that mixing red and white makes pink, encourage her to mix a small amount on her plate. Then have her use a cotton swab to write the word *pink* on a sheet of white paper.

pink

Pink Snacks

Youngsters will be tickled pink over these snacks!

- cookies or cupcakes with pink frosting
- strawberry ice cream
- strawberry milk shakes
- pink lemonade
- pink grapefruit

I Love Pink

Sing the song below with your youngsters. Then encourage each child to name a favorite pink object.

(sung to the tune of "Three Blind Mice")

I love pink. I love pink.
That's what I think. That's what I think.
I love this color so much I could shout
About a pink piglet and his tiny snout
Or pink bubble gum that I can't do without.
I love pink.

Ten Little Pigs

Here piggy, piggy! Gather ten youngsters and have them stand in a row. Give each child his pig puppet (see "Piggy Puppet" on page 100). Lead students in singing the song, prompting each child to hold up his puppet when indicated. That's ten little piggies!

(sung to the tune of "Ten Little Indians")

One little, two little, three pink piggies,
Four little, five little, six pink piggies,
Seven little, eight little, nine pink piggies,
Ten little pink piggies!

Pink Printing

What a perfectly pink way to practice color word recognition! Make or obtain a batch of pink play dough to place at a center. Program several 9" x 12" sheets of pink construction paper with the word *pink*. Laminate the sheets for durability. Then invite several youngsters to the center. Encourage each youngster to roll pieces of dough into logs and then lay them on the letters to form the word. Finally, have each child name the letters. P-I-N-K—that's pink!

Color Parade

Plan a color parade with your youngsters! Divide students into ten groups, with one or more children in each group. Then assign each group a different color. Have one child in each color group carry an appropriately colored sign labeled with the color word. Use the following ideas to make costumes and additional props. Then teach the song on page 105 and let the marching begin!

Red: Have a child pull a red wagon with a basketful of apples. Have other youngsters carry stop signs and wear red capes.

Blue: Encourage students to wear blue jeans. In addition, have youngsters carry blue bookbags or bluebird puppets (see "Bluebird Puppet" on page 68).

Green: Invite students to wear green sweaters and hats. In addition, have them carry green leaves, green shamrock cutouts, or green turtle puppets (see "Tinted Turtles" on page 72).

Yellow: Encourage children to wear yellow shirts and sunglasses. Also have them carry yellow beach towels or sun puppets (see "Sunshine Puppet" on page 76).

Orange: Have students carry orange plastic pumpkins filled with carrots and wear orange headbands. Also invite youngsters to carry orange fish puppets (see "Goldfish Bowl" on page 80).

Purple: Invite students to wear purple shirts. In addition, have youngsters carry purple flowers.

Brown: Have each child wear a brown vest (see "Brown Vest" on page 88). In addition, have youngsters carry brown teddy bears.

Black: Encourage students to wear black clothing. Also invite them to carry bat puppets (see "Black Bat Puppets" on page 93).

White: Invite students to wear white T-shirts. Have them carry white snowflake cutouts or snowpal crafts (see "Glittering Snowpals" on page 96).

Pink: Encourage youngsters to wear pink hats or headbands and carry pink flowers. Also invite students to carry pig puppets (see "Piggy Puppet" on page 100).

Color Parade Song

(sung to the tune of
"When Johnny Comes Marching Home")

The colors are marching into town. Hooray! Hooray!
The colors are marching in a great big color parade.
The reds have stop signs; they look so keen.
Then come blues with their bags and jeans.
Oh, we're so glad the colors could come today.

The colors are marching into town. Hooray! Hooray!
The greens are waving turtles as they march our way.
Then come yellows, each with a sun.
And oranges bring carrots for everyone.
Oh, we're so glad the colors could come today.

The colors are marching into town. Hooray! Hooray!
The purples wave flowers as they march our way.
Here comes brown with some teddy bears.
And black has bats that might give a scare.
Oh, we're so glad the colors could come today.

The colors are marching into town. Hooray! Hooray!
The colors are marching in a great big color parade.
Next comes white with jolly snowmen.
Last comes pink with pigs in pens.
Oh, we're so glad the colors could come today.

Apple Pattern
Use with "A Basketful of Apples" on page 64 and "Writing on Red" on page 67.

Stop Sign Pattern
Use with "Eight-Sided Signs" on page 33, "Stop on Red" on page 65, and "Writing on Red" on page 67.

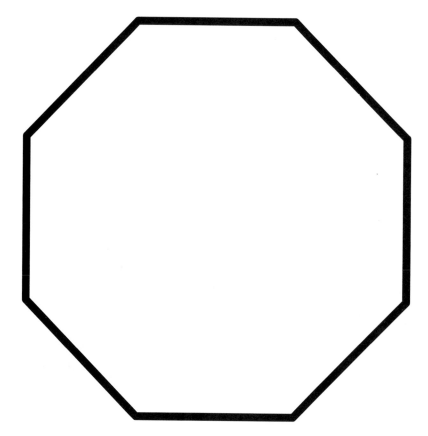

Bluebird Pattern
Use with "Bluebird Puppet" on page 68.

Ribbon Pattern
Use with "Blueberry Toss" on page 69.

Turtle Patterns

Use with "Tinted Turtles" on page 72 and "Spotted Turtles" on page 73.

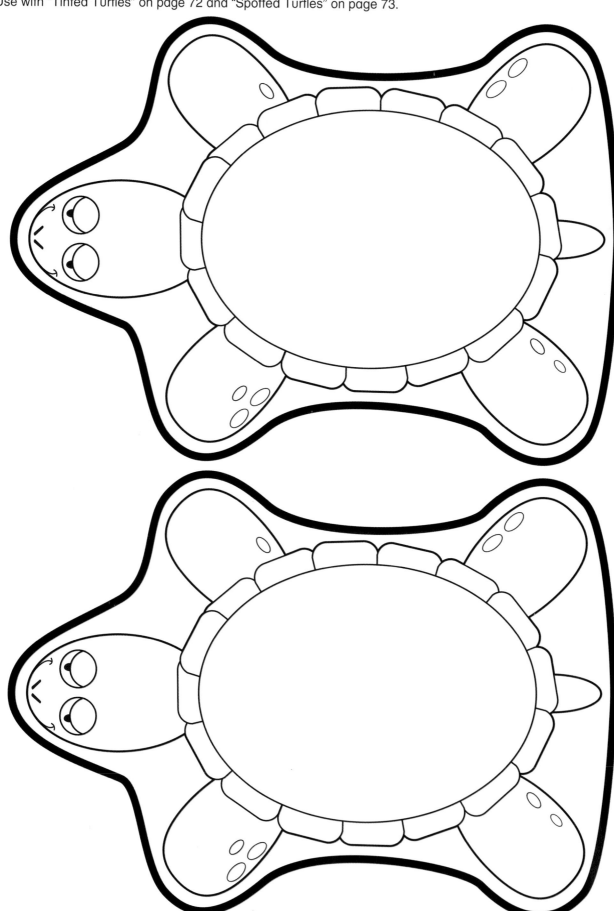

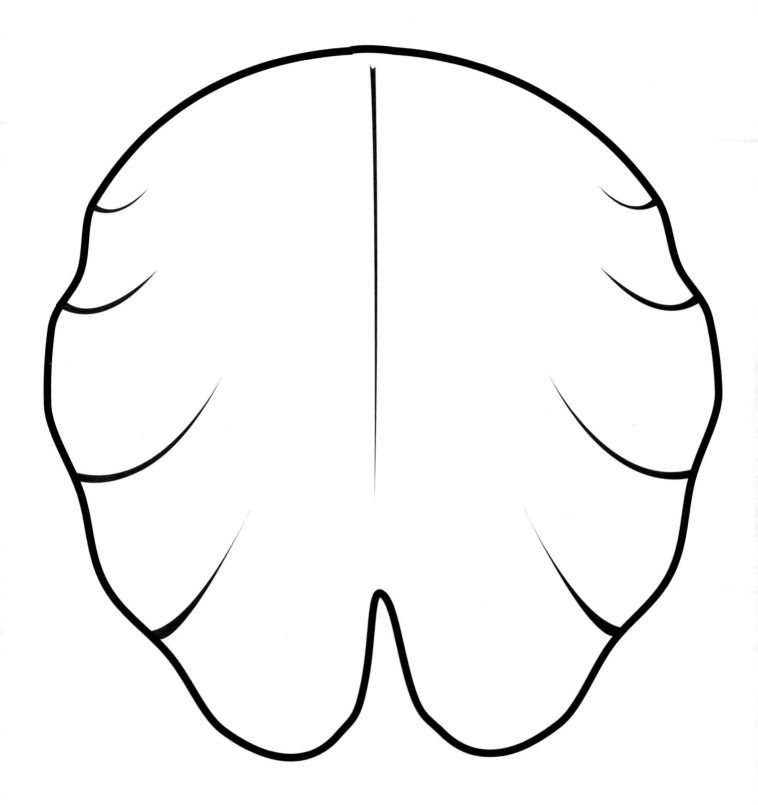

Sun Pattern
Use with "Sunshine Puppet" on page 76.

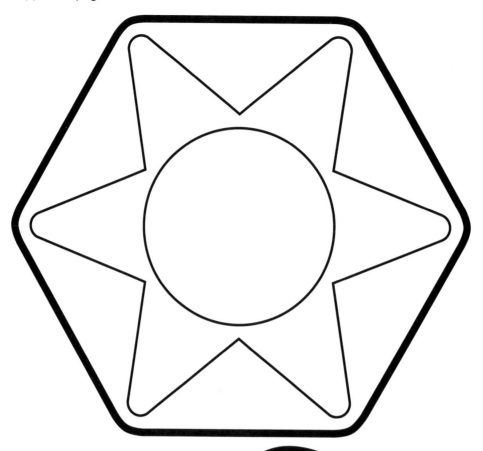

Duck Pattern
Use with "Ducks on a Pond" on page 76 and
"Ducks in a Row" on page 77.

110

Pumpkin Pattern
Use with "Pleasingly Orange Pumpkins" on page 80.

Fish Pattern
Use with "Goldfish Bowl" on page 80.

Flower Pattern
Use with "Yellow Daffodils" on page 76 and "Purple Posies" on page 84.

Cow Pattern
Use with "Purple Cow Puppet" on page 87.

Bear Pattern
Use with "Fuzzy Wuzzy Bears" on page 88.

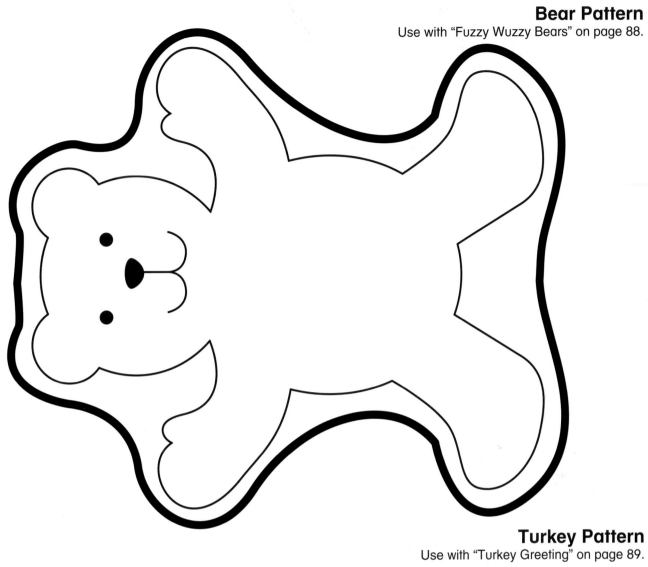

Turkey Pattern
Use with "Turkey Greeting" on page 89.

Bat Pattern
Use with "Black Bat Puppets" on page 93.

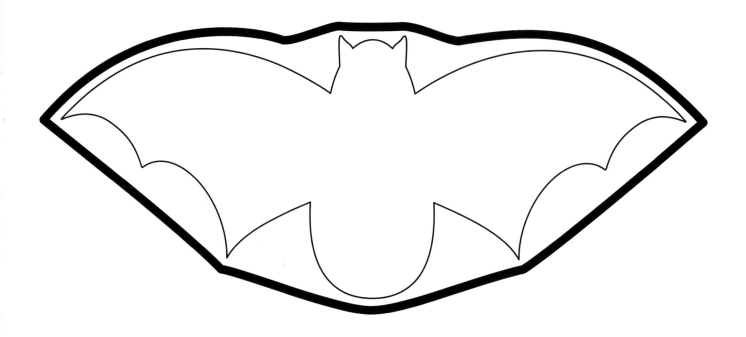

Cat Pattern
Use with "Five Black Cats" on page 93.

Snowpal Pattern

Use with "Glittering Snowpals" on page 96.

Bunny Pattern

Use with "Four White Bunnies" on page 97.

Pig Pattern

Use with "Piggy Puppet" on page 100 and "Lacing Pigs" on page 101.

Tulip Pattern

Use with "Pink-Tinted Tulips" on page 100.

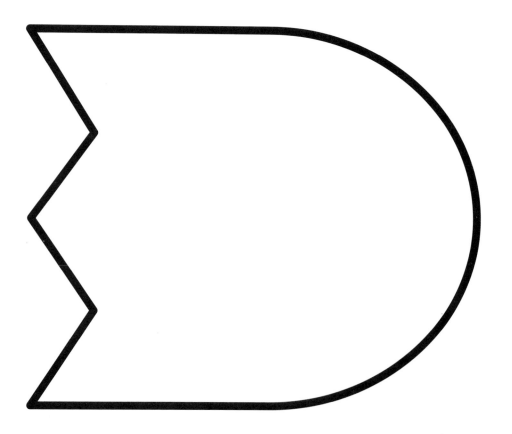

116

Shapes

Circles

Circle Fun

Combine circle awareness with art in the following fun activities!

- Invite each child to practice cutting skills by using scissors to cut out the circle pattern on a copy of page 140.
- Give each child a construction paper copy of page 140 and various colors of bingo daubers. Invite her to pretend she's filling a gumball machine and to daub circles onto the cutout. When she's finished, help her glue on a base cut from construction paper.
- Give each child markers and a circle cut from a construction paper copy of page 140. Invite her to decorate her circle. Then help her tape on a craft stick handle to make a bright, breezy fan.

Printing Circles

Add tactile fun to children's circle awareness, and you're bound to get great artistic response! Set out several different kinds of circle stamps, such as jar lids, sponges cut into circles, and circular rubber stamps. Prepare shallow trays of washable tempera paint. Give each child a sheet of construction paper and invite him to stamp it with circles. Encourage him to try each stamp for a variety of circles. When the paint is dry, help him trace the circles with his finger while softly saying the word *circle*.

Shadow Match

Put circles in the spotlight while building matching and size discrimination skills. Select several child-safe objects with circular bottoms, such as a plastic cup, a round cookie cutter, a paper plate, and a plastic bowl. Trace each object's bottom onto black construction paper and cut out the resulting circle to represent a shadow. Glue the shadows onto a large sheet of tagboard and place it in a center with the objects. Invite children at this center to match each object with its shadow.

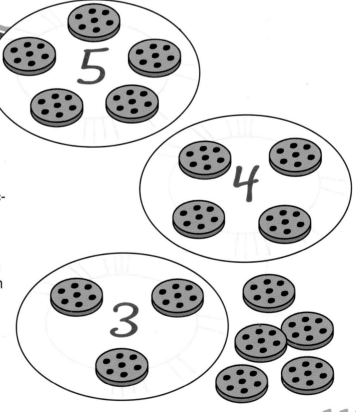

Cookie Math

This mouthwatering math activity is lots of fun! Label each of six paper plates with a different numeral from 1 to 6. Cut 21 round cookie shapes from tan construction paper or craft foam. Add chocolate chip details with a permanent black marker. Point out to children that the cookie manipulatives and plates are circles. Next, encourage youngsters to take turns reading a numeral on a plate and then placing the appropriate number of round cookies on the plate. Afterward, you may wish to serve youngsters cookie treats for all their hard work!

119

Circle Movement Fun

Get your little ones into circles with these simple and energetic activities!

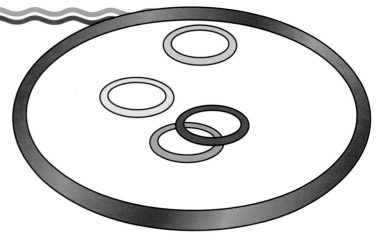

- Place large plastic hoops on the floor and invite children to take turns jumping in and out of the circles.
- Place one large plastic hoop on the floor and invite each child to take a turn tossing in small flying discs or plastic rings.
- Set up a ringtoss game. Help children understand that rings are circles.

Dramatic Play

Enjoy a little theater in the round with these creative additions to your dramatic-play center.

- plastic and paper plates in a variety of sizes and colors
- bangle bracelets
- round hats
- collapsible camping cups
- round containers and lids
- pretend cakes and pizzas

Circle Snack Ideas

Youngsters are sure to get a taste for circles when you serve these round snacks!

- round cookies
- round crackers with cream cheese and sliced olives
- ring-shaped cereal pieces
- sliced cucumbers and tomatoes
- English muffin pizzas with pepperoni
- pancakes
- mini bagels
- doughnuts
- cooked pasta wheels

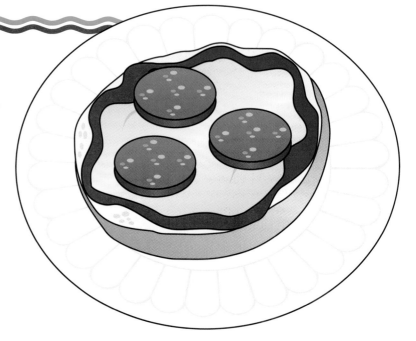

I'm a Circle

Enjoy a rousing sing-along with this little ditty! After singing the song together, invite children to name objects that are circles.

(sung to the tune of "Three Blind Mice")

I'm a circle. I'm a circle.
Round and fat, round and fat.
I can be a clock or a ball.
I could roll when I fall.
I have no corners at all.
I'm a circle.

Tracing Circles

These designs are not only pretty to look at, but they will also help develop letter formation skills. Cut several different sizes of circles from cardboard. Put the circles, drawing paper, and an assortment of markers, pencils, and crayons in a center. A child places a circle on her paper, traces around it, and then colors it. She continues in this manner, overlapping circles as desired to create a pleasing design.

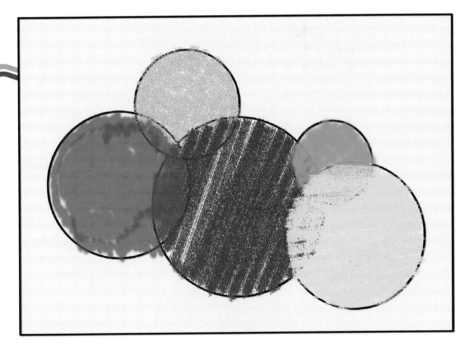

Squares

Cutting Squares

A square is a square, no matter the size! Using the square pattern on page 141 as a guide, cut a square from copy paper for each child. Have each child fold his square in half and then in half again. Direct him to unfold his square and count the four squares inside. Then invite him to draw a picture on the paper, making sure that elements of his picture fall in each quadrant. Give him a pair of scissors and help him carefully cut along the fold lines to create a four-piece square puzzle. Place the pieces in a resealable plastic bag. Then encourage each child to take his puzzle home to share with his family!

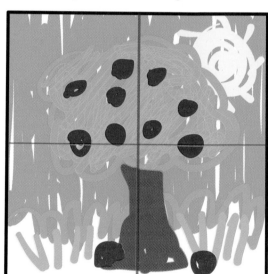

Mosaics

Reinforce the square shape with this pretty project! In advance, cut a supply of colorful tissue paper into one-inch squares. Also cut a six-inch square from white construction paper for each child. Provide bowls of diluted white glue and old paintbrushes. Give each youngster her construction paper square and have her identify the shape. Then encourage her to paint glue on the square. Next, invite her to carefully arrange tissue paper squares side by side to cover the glue. When the glue is dry, display the mosaics in a large square shape. Beautiful!

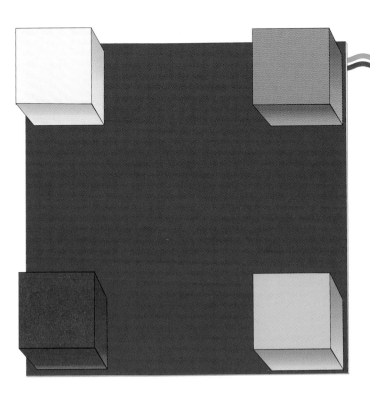

Block Directions

Hang out in the block center and have some fun with squares and positional words! Set out a square of colorful poster board and four square blocks. Working with one child at a time, have him examine the blocks. Lead him to understand that the face of the block has four equal sides, which makes it a square. Point out that the poster board is also a square. Then ask the child to perform the following actions:

- Put a block in each corner of the large square.
- Put a stack of blocks in the middle.
- Put four blocks along one of the sides.
- Put a block inside the large square. Put another block beside it.

Find the Square

Help your little ones get a feel for squares with this sensational idea! In advance, cut a variety of shapes from cardboard, making sure there are several squares. Put all the shapes into a pillowcase. Invite a child to reach into the bag without looking, feel the shapes, and pull out a square. Repeat the activity with different children as desired. For a more challenging activity, put three-dimensional objects into the pillowcase. Suggestions include a round bracelet, a square block, a triangle instrument, a rectangular ruler, and a heart-shaped candy box.

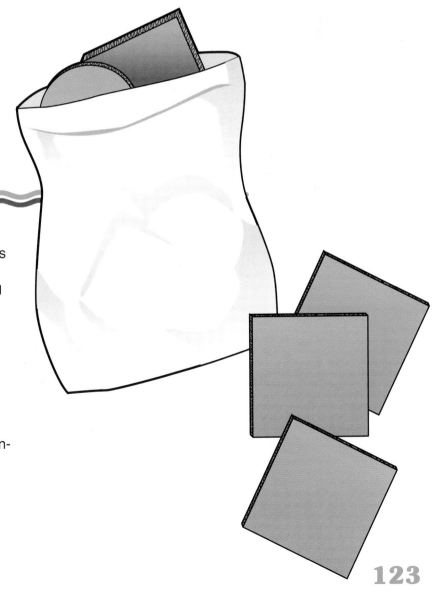

Square Moves

Pick and choose from the following movement ideas to help your active little learners comprehend squares!

- Make a masking tape square on the floor. Invite children to walk, tiptoe, march, and dance along the lines.
- Have four children lay down and form a square with their bodies.
- Use chalk to draw a series of squares on a paved surface. Invite children to hop in and out of the squares.

Dramatic Play

Be sure to include plenty of square objects in your dramatic-play center. Consider adding some of the following items:

- square baking pans
- square potholders
- square napkins
- square boxes and containers
- clothing with square buttons and buckles
- square purses and accessories
- graduation mortarboards

Scrumptious Squares

These squares are fun and delicious, so why not try a few today!

- cheese cubes and squares
- square crackers
- square cereal pieces
- graham cracker halves
- sandwiches cut into squares
- square waffles
- brownies cut into squares

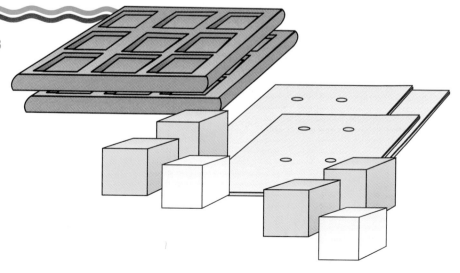

124

I'm a Square

Enjoy a rousing sing-along with this little ditty! After singing the song together, invite children to name objects that are squares.

(sung to the tune of "Are You Sleeping")

I'm a square. I'm a square.
That's no lie. I'll tell you why.
I have four sides.
All are the same size.
I'm a square. I'm a square.

Square Book

Read all about squares with this class book! Give each child a nine-inch white paper square. As a group, discuss objects that can be square, such as windows, tables, boxes, crackers, and so forth. Next, encourage each child to draw a square object on her paper. Have her write the object's name under her drawing, providing help as necessary. Then help the child mount her page on a ten-inch colorful construction paper square. Stack all the pages and bind them between two covers. Title the book "Squares" and read it aloud with student help. Later, place the book in your class library for continued enjoyment.

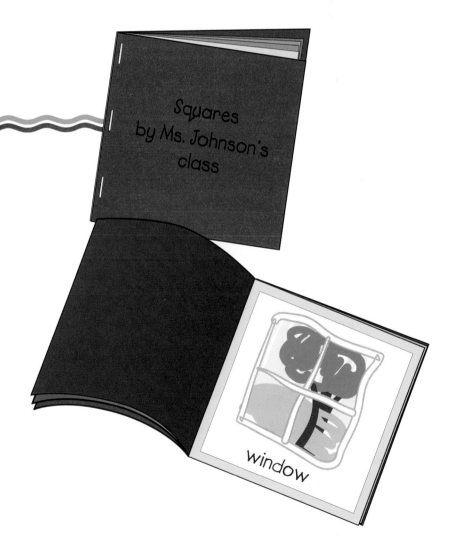

Squares
by Ms. Johnson's
class

window

Triangles

Triangle Puppet People

Let's have a puppet show! Give each child a construction paper copy of page 142; then help her cut out the triangle pattern. Invite her to add facial features and details to her triangle with crayons or markers. Then help her tape a craft stick handle to the back to make a puppet. Encourage groups of three children to make up puppet shows featuring their triangle people.

Winning Pennants

Oh boy! What a great-looking pennant! Explain to students that pennants are triangular flags; then tell them that they're going to have a chance to make their very own! Give each child a construction paper copy of page 142. Have her cut out the triangle pattern, providing help as needed. Encourage students to decorate their cutouts with a variety of colorful triangles. Then tape a paint stick to the back to make a pennant. Snazzy!

Three-Sided Sorting

This easy idea is sure to help youngsters recognize and identify triangles! In advance, cut a variety of triangles, squares, and circles from brightly colored paper. Spread the shapes in your small-group area and have several students examine them. Draw students' attention to one of the triangles and ask them what they notice about it. How many sides does it have? How many corners? What color is the shape? Does size or color make a difference? Help students grasp that every triangle has three sides and corners, no matter what its size or color. Have students help you pick out all the triangles. Encourage them to discuss their work. Then prompt youngsters to sort just the triangles by size, color, or another attribute.

Flannelboard Triangle Fun

Cute little pumpkins with faces made entirely of triangles? Sure! Cut five pumpkin shapes from orange felt, using the pattern from page 111 as a guide. Also cut fifteen small black triangles from black felt. Place the pumpkins on your flannelboard; then add three triangles to each one to resemble eyes and a nose. Read the following rhyme aloud, removing the triangles from each pumpkin when indicated. Invite each of five volunteers to replace the triangles on a different pumpkin. No doubt youngsters will ask for several rounds of this fun activity!

Five little pumpkins with ten triangle eyes
And five triangle noses—what a surprise!
When I take them off, can you replace
All of the triangles on each pumpkin face?

Triangle Moves

Get in shape with this assortment of kid-pleasing kinesthetic activities!

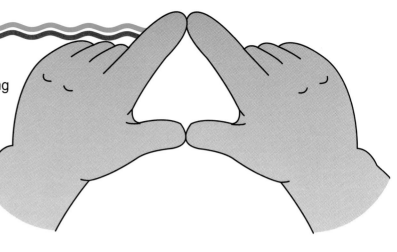

- Have groups of three youngsters lie on the floor and use their bodies to make triangles.
- Demonstrate how to make a finger triangle using your thumbs and forefingers. Encourage children to copy you; then have them explore other ways to make triangles with their bodies.
- Mark three corners on your playground. Then lead your students in a parade to each corner, encouraging them to identify the shape of their walking route.

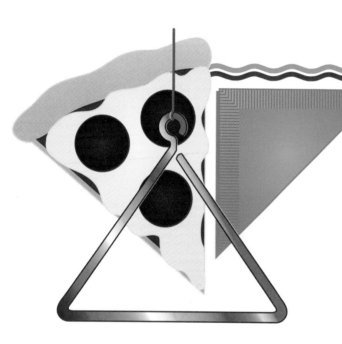

Dramatic Play

Be sure to include plenty of triangular objects for exploration in your dramatic-play center. Consider adding some of the following items:

- triangular pizza and pie containers
- play foods such as cheese, pizza, and pie wedges
- tricorn hats
- triangle musical instruments
- napkins folded into triangles
- scarves and bandanas folded into triangles

Tasty Triangles

Nibbling a few of these three-cornered treats will certainly help your youngsters internalize triangles!

- cheese and ham slices cut into triangles
- triangular chips (such as nacho chips)
- triangular crackers
- sandwiches cut into triangles
- turnovers
- pizza slices
- pie slices

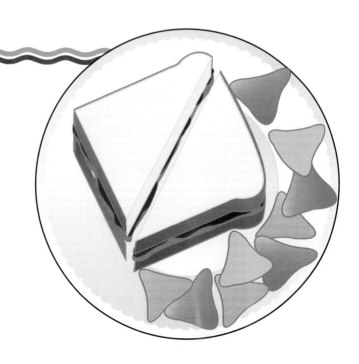

I Love Triangles

Enjoy a rousing sing-along with this little ditty! After singing the song together, invite children to name objects that are triangles.

(sung to the tune of "Three Blind Mice")

I love triangles. I love triangles.
Yes I do. Yes I do.
They have three sides; that is true.
They can be sails on the ocean blue.
They are chips and sandwiches too.
I love triangles.

Triangle Picture Book

Encourage creative thinking with this adorable class-made book! For each child, draw a black triangle on a sheet of white paper. Invite her to study her triangle and think about what it could become. For example, a triangle could become an evergreen tree, the roof of a house, or an ice-cream cone. Then have her draw to transform her triangle into an illustration. Help each child write a sentence about her triangle picture. Bind the pages between construction paper covers to create a class book. Then enlist students to help read the book aloud. Wow—look at all the nifty triangles!

A triangle can hold a bunch of flowers.

Our Triangle Book by Ms. Warren's class

Rectangles

City Dwellings

Many city buildings resemble rectangles, and city homes are no exception! Cut out a class supply of colorful construction paper rectangles, using the pattern on page 143 as a guide if desired. Also cut out a supply of yellow construction paper strips. Explain to your students that the rectangle represents a city building, and it needs windows so the people who live there can see outside. Encourage each child to cut rectangles from her strip. Then have her glue them onto the building. Display the completed buildings on a bulletin board with other rectangular cityscape embellishments such as sidewalks and traffic lights. Rectangles are right at home in the city!

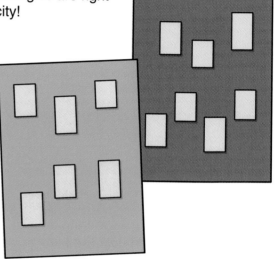

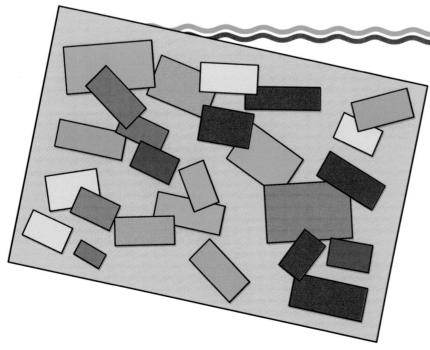

Rectangular Placemats

A little spark of creativity is all that's needed to transform ordinary rectangles into art! In advance, cut out a variety of rectangles from colorful construction paper. Give each child a 12" x 18" sheet of construction paper and access to the precut rectangles. Then invite him to glue the shapes to his paper to create a collage. As he works, have him describe the shapes. Guide him to notice that each shape has four corners and two sets of equal sides. Explain that each shape is a rectangle. When each child has completed his collage, laminate it to make a placemat suitable for snacktime, lunchtime, or anytime.

Rectangle Flags

Your youngsters will be eager to wave these rectangular banners high! To prepare, obtain several pictures of flags. Set out a variety of craft supplies, such as paper and ribbon scraps, glue, glitter, markers, and crayons. Also provide scissors and glue. Show students the flag pictures and discuss their rectangular shape. Explain that a flag represents a country, state, or special group. Then let each child create her own flag on a sheet of construction paper with the provided craft supplies. Encourage her to design the flag with drawings that are special to her. Afterward, invite each child to decribe her flag to the class. Then mount the flags on a bulletin board or wall for a pleasing display!

Searching for Rectangles

Challenge little learners to recognize rectangles. In advance, place a variety of objects shaped like squares, triangles, and circles in a rectangular box. Then, during a circle time, have youngsters help you sort the objects by shape. When they have finished, point out that the box is the only rectangle. Then discuss the rectangle's attributes and send each child to look around the room for a rectangular object. If the object is small, such as a book or ruler, have the child put it in the box. If it is large, such as a door or table, have the child stand beside the object. Wow! Look at all the rectangles in the room!

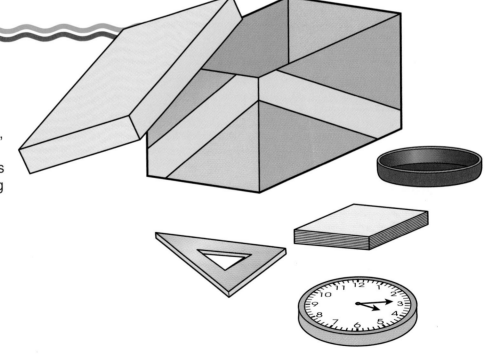

Magic Carpet Rectangles

When youngsters learn about rectangles with this movement activity, they're sure to have lots of fun! Scatter a class supply of rectangular carpet samples around your room. Ask each child to stand on a rectangle. Then give movement directions such as the following:

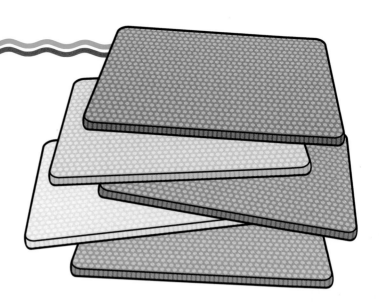

- Jump onto your rectangle; then jump off.
- Stand on the two long sides of your rectangle.
- Stand on the two short sides of your rectangle.
- Touch all four corners of your rectangle at the same time.
- Tiptoe around your rectangle.
- Crawl around your rectangle.

Dramatic Play

Be sure to include plenty of rectangular objects in your dramatic-play center. Consider adding some of the following items:

- rectangular trays
- rectangular placemats and tablecloths
- empty rectangular food packages
- small rectangular suitcases
- clothing with rectangular pockets
- rectangular scarves
- rectangular purses
- rectangular boxes

Rectangular Snacks

These rectangles are fun and delicious, so try a few today!

- rectangular crackers or cookies
- graham crackers (either one-fourth of a cracker or a whole cracker)
- sugar wafer cookies
- crispy rice cereal treats cut into rectangles
- sandwich meats and cheeses cut into rectangles
- ice-cream sandwiches
- granola bars

I'm a Big Rectangle

Enjoy a rousing sing-along with this little ditty! After singing the song together, invite children to name objects that are shaped like rectangles.

(sung to the tune of "I'm a Little Teapot")

I'm a big rectangle, can't you see?
I have two sets of sides on me.
Two are short, and two are long.
Both are straight and both are strong!

Making Rectangles

Strengthen little fingers while preparing youngsters to write with a few of these activities!

- Provide each child with crayons, rectangular tracers, and paper. Invite him to trace around the rectangles and then draw a few rectangles by himself.
- Make sets of four dots on small sheets of paper. Have each child draw straight lines to connect the dots to form a rectangle.
- Provide a supply of craft sticks in different sizes. Encourage each child to arrange the craft sticks into rectangles.
- Program play dough workmats with a variety of rectangles. Invite each child to roll play dough into narrow lengths and use it to outline the rectangles.

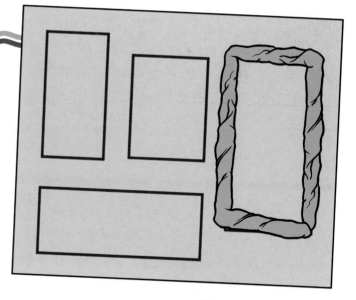

Ovals

Oval Collages

These pretty collages are a great way to introduce ovals! To begin, have each child brush brightly colored tempera paints over a sheet of paper. When the paint is dry, help him cut ovals from the paper. Then provide him with a colorful construction paper oval to use as a collage base (use the pattern on page 144 as a guide). Invite him to glue his painted ovals to the base in a pleasing collage arrangement. As each child works on his collage, encourage him to notice the unique oval shape. When the glue is dry, have him trace each oval as he softly says the word *oval.* That's a lot of ovals!

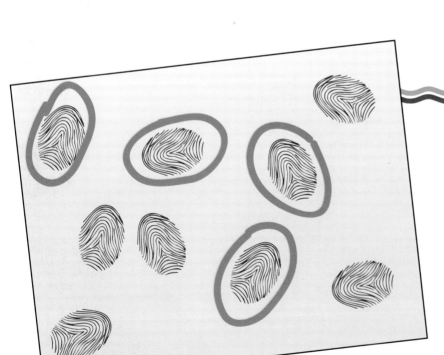

Fingerprint Ovals

It's true—ovals are always at your fingertips! Give each child a sheet of paper and access to an ink pad with washable ink. Demonstrate how to press a finger on the ink pad and then make a fingerprint on paper. For fun, show her how to turn the paper (or her hand) to make horizontal or vertical ovals. When each child has made several fingerprints, encourage her to draw an oval around each print that resembles an oval.

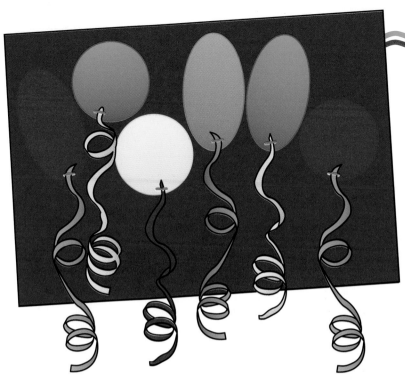

Balloons for Sale!

Which shape balloon will your little ones choose? Ovals, of course! In advance, cut a variety of oval and round shapes from red, yellow, green, and blue felt. Staple a length of curling ribbon to each cutout to form a balloon. Next, arrange the balloons in a bunch on a flannelboard and gather a small group of students. Review the oval shape with your youngsters. Say the rhyme below and then invite each child, in turn, to choose an oval balloon from the bunch.

Balloons for sale! Balloons for sale!
Red, yellow, green, and blue.
Balloons for sale! Balloons for sale!
Which one will you choose?

Oval Racetrack

This race-inspired game is sure to rev youngsters' engines while reinforcing oval-recognition skills! Draw a large oval racetrack on a sheet of black tagboard; then add a start/finish line with yellow paint. Also use paint to section the track as shown. When the paint is dry, cut out the racetrack. Gather four toy cars and a large foam die. Give each of four children a car and have the students place the cars on the starting line. Discuss the shape of the racetrack and invite students to describe any oval racetracks they have seen. Then invite one child to roll the die and move his car the corresponding number of spaces. Play continues with each child, in turn, until everyone has moved around the track and crossed the finish line. Vroom!

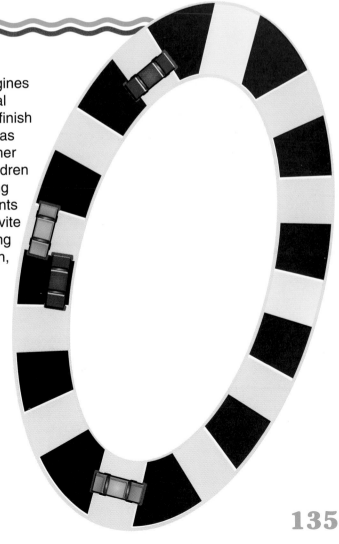

135

Moving Ovals

These energetic activities are bound to get the wiggles out while reinforcing oval-awareness skills!

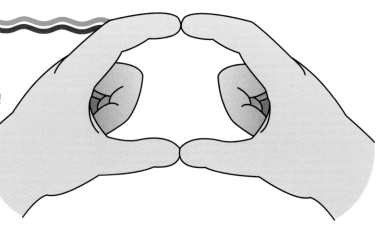

- Have your students make finger ovals by touching their thumbs and forefingers together as shown.
- Place a length of rope on the floor in the shape of an oval. Encourage small groups of students to move around the oval in a variety of ways, including crawling, hopping, tiptoeing, and skipping.
- Tape a set of large gray oval cutouts to the floor to represent stepping stones. Have each child hop from one stepping stone to the next, whispering the word *oval* each time he steps on one.

Playing With Ovals

Be sure to include plenty of oval objects for exploration in your dramatic-play center. Consider adding some of the following:

- oval placemats
- plastic oval dishes
- plastic oval frames
- toy oval sunglasses
- belts with oval buckles
- oval accessories such as purses

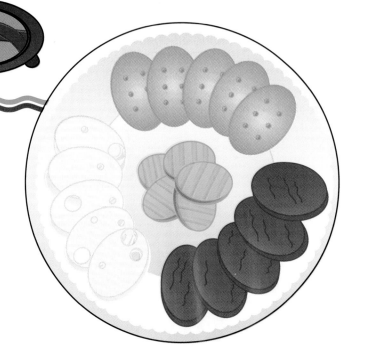

Eating Ovals

Munch and crunch your way through oval recognition with a few of these tasty snack ideas!

- oval-shaped crackers and cookies
- oval pickle slices
- cheese and meat slices cut with oval cookie cutters

I'm a Little Oval

Enjoy a rousing sing-along with this little ditty! After singing the song together, invite children to name objects that are ovals.

(sung to the tune of "I'm a Little Teapot")

I'm a little oval, not quite round.
I'm not the same all around.
I'm kind of squashed, and that's not all.
I won't roll if I should fall.

Oval Writing

Strengthen youngsters' little fingers while preparing them to write with a few of these activities!

- Set out a shallow pan containing a layer of sand. Invite each child, in turn, to use a fingertip to draw ovals in the sand. A gentle shake erases the ovals for the next child!
- Give each child paper and markers. Have her picture an oval racetrack and then practice drawing her own.
- Squeeze a small amount of colored hair gel (or tempera paint) into a sandwich-sized resealable plastic bag. Push the air out, seal the bag, and then tape the seal closed. Encourage each child to use her finger to draw an oval on the bag and then smooth out the gel. Have her repeat the process several times.

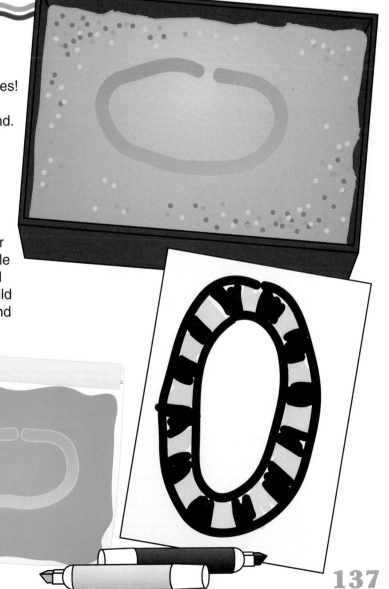

Shape Parade

Plan a shape parade with your youngsters! Divide students into five groups and assign each group a different shape to represent. Use the following ideas to make costumes and props. Then teach the song on page 139 and let the marching begin!

Circles: Wear polka-dot clothing, carry large plastic hoops, and make round crowns from sentence strips. Have one child carry a large poster board circle.

Squares: Wear square bandanas or scarves and carry square blocks and square mosaics (see "Mosaics" on page 122). Have one child carry a large poster board square.

Triangles: Wear tricorn hats and carry triangle instruments and pennants (see "Winning Pennants" on page 126). Have one child carry a large poster board triangle.

Rectangles: Pull a rectangular wagon filled with rectangular blocks and books. Wave the rectangular flags from page 131. Have one child carry a large poster board rectangle.

Ovals: Wear oval toy sunglasses and carry oval collages (see "Oval Collages" on page 134). Have one child carry a large poster board oval.

Shape Parade Song

(sung to the tune of
"When Johnny Comes Marching Home")

The shapes are marching into town. Hooray! Hooray!
The shapes are marching in a great big shape parade.
First come circles big and round.
Then the squares come into town.
Oh, we're so glad the shapes could come today.

The shapes are marching into town Hooray! Hooray!
The triangles are ringing as they come our way.
The rectangles are marching by.
Here come the ovals waving hi.
Oh, we're so glad the shapes could come today.

Circle Pattern
Use with "Circle Fun" on page 118.

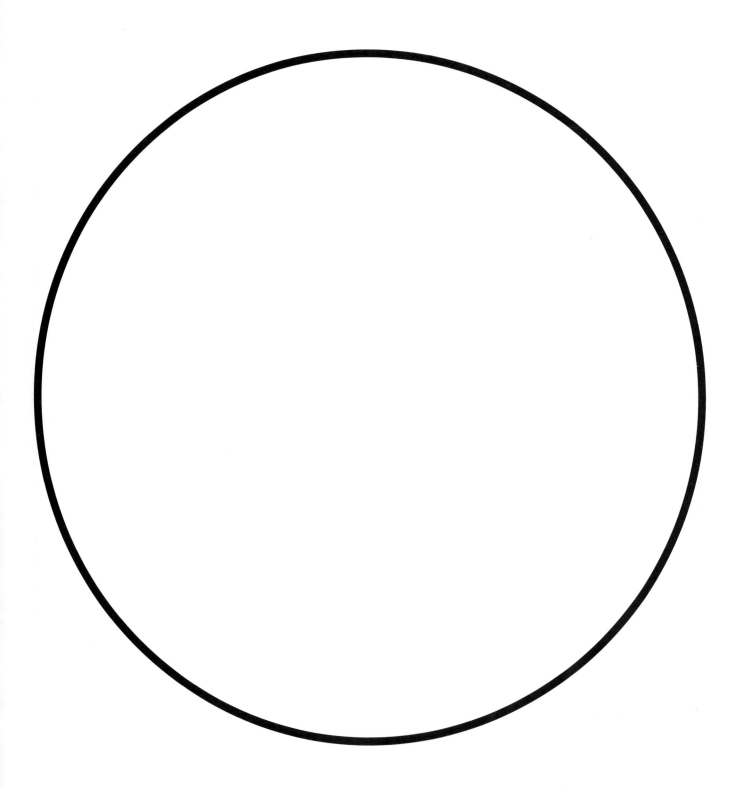

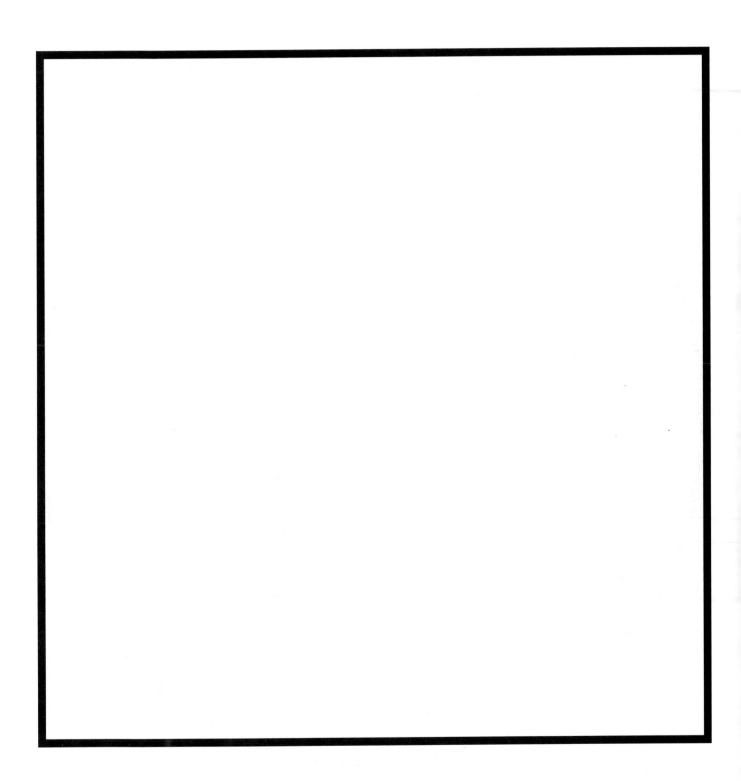

Triangle Pattern
Use with "Triangle Puppet People" and "Winning Pennants" on page 126.

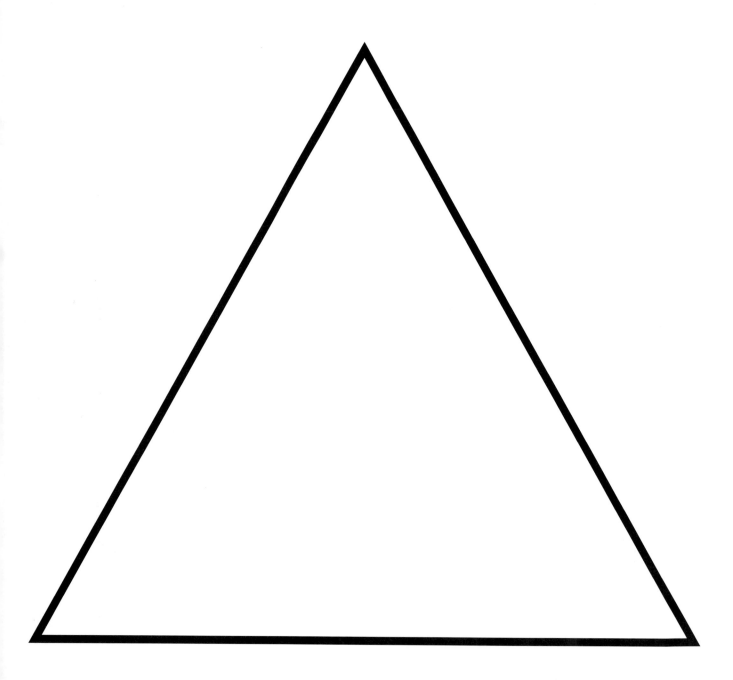

Oval Pattern

Use with "Oval Collages" on page 134.

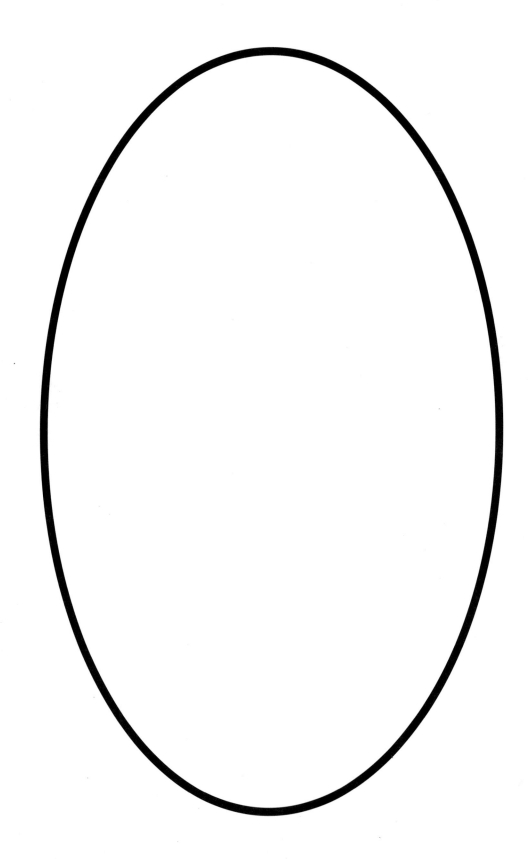